D1695017

Serpentine Gallery Pavilion 2007
Olafur Eliasson and Kjetil Thorsen

Serpentine Gallery
Lars Müller Publishers

Contents

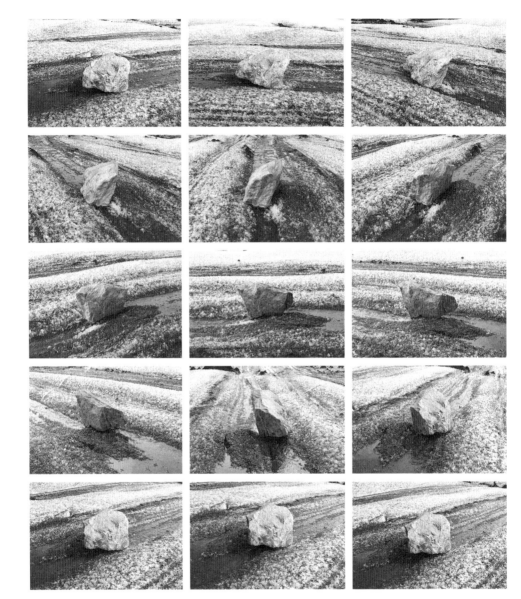

Olafur Eliasson, *The glacier surfer,* 2007

Bloomberg is delighted to sponsor the Serpentine Gallery Pavilion 2007, designed by Olafur Eliasson and Kjetil Thorsen. This year the Pavilion reflects Bloomberg's culture by creating a dynamic experimental space to engage and inspire the public.

Bloomberg's sponsorship of the Serpentine Gallery Pavilion 2007 reflects the company's sustained commitment to the arts and builds on Bloomberg's long association with the Serpentine Gallery's exhibition, architecture and education programmes. The unique elements of this alliance with the Serpentine Gallery help Bloomberg meet its philanthropic goals of supporting cutting-edge talent, providing public access to the arts and engaging diverse audiences in the creative process.

As a leading global financial information services company, Bloomberg is deeply committed to education and creativity, and to expanding access to art, science and the humanities. Through support of educational and cultural institutions worldwide, Bloomberg fosters a broad range of creative initiatives – from exhibitions and audio tour programmes to student fellowships and public art installations – that promote public awareness and appreciation of the arts and encourage higher education.

Lex Fenwick, *Chief Executive Officer*

Bloomberg

Directors' Foreword

The Serpentine Gallery Pavilion commission is unique worldwide. An ongoing programme of temporary structures for the Serpentine Gallery's lawn, it presents the work of an internationally acclaimed practitioner who, at the time of the Serpentine Gallery's invitation, has not completed a building in the UK.

The annual architectural commission sits beside the other strands of the Serpentine's programming: exhibitions, education and public programmes. We believe it to be the best forum to display architecture rather than the drawings, plans and models frequently used in architecture exhibitions, which can end up focusing more on display and technology than on the buildings themselves. It is also a process that parallels the way in which we commission and exhibit art: it builds upon a long history of artists' commissions that have included radical interventions in the actual structure of the building, as well as drastic gestures and display features within the galleries, in order to alter the perception of the Serpentine and its surroundings. The intention of the commission is to show people the extraordinary richness of contemporary architecture and allow them to compare their personal experience of one Pavilion with the next, and thus to become engaged and involved in architecture.

The Pavilion architects to date are Zaha Hadid, 2000; Daniel Libeskind with Arup, 2001; Toyo Ito with Arup, 2002; Oscar Niemeyer, 2003; MVRDV with Arup, 2004 – (unrealised); Álvaro Siza and Eduardo Souto de Moura with Cecil Balmond – Arup, 2005; and Rem Koolhaas and Cecil Balmond, with Arup, 2006. The brief given to the architects is that the Pavilion should be 'a functioning example of their work'. It is a temporary and demountable, which could be sold on or even rolled out as an edition or multiple. Each Pavilion, from commission to completion, takes around six months. We have found that this fast-forward programme, opposed to the usual protracted time it takes to design and build, while undoubtedly challenging, provokes designers into experimentation, spurs the expansion of their ideas, and results in the most direct realisation of their immediate concepts.

The Serpentine Gallery Pavilion 2007 is designed by the internationally acclaimed artist Olafur Eliasson (Berlin/Copenhagen) and the award-winning architect Kjetil Thorsen, of the architectural practice Snøhetta (Oslo). This collaboration is the continuation of a creative and productive working relationship between the artist and architect that began formally in 2005 with the making of a large-scale, site-specific work by Eliasson that will be installed in the foyer of the new National Opera House, Oslo, which was designed by Snøhetta in 2000 and is due for completion in 2008.

The expansion of the Serpentine Pavilion design team to include a visual artist is not new and the collaboration of two designers has developed from previous years' Pavilions, most notably in 2005, when two architects, Álvaro Siza and Eduardo Souto de Moura – who, like Eliasson and Thorsen, had a pre-existing creative partnership, worked together on the annual architectural commission.

In 2006, Pavilion designers Rem Koolhaas and Cecil Balmond, with Arup, collaborated with the artist Thomas Demand, whose solo exhibition in the Serpentine Gallery was concurrent with the Pavilion. The objective was to create an explicit link between the Serpentine's art and architecture programmes and the many meetings involving the architect and artist resulted in a visual motif that appeared in both the Gallery and the Pavilion. For his exhibition, Demand designed a series of ivy-pattern wallpapers, developed from the subject matter of one of his photographs, that covered the walls of the Serpentine's galleries, emphasising its domestic scale. This pattern was manipulated and reproduced on a large-scale frieze that hung beneath the inflatable hemispheric void above the Pavilion's amphitheatre. This introduced into the ethereal Pavilion space both the geometry of the Gallery and the mode of still observation evident in Demand's work.

The overarching interest in spatial questions explored in Eliasson's artistic practice has resulted in an increasing engagement with architectural projects. These include a rooftop extension at

8

Serpentine Gallery Pavilion 2000
Designed by Zaha Hadid

Serpentine Gallery Pavilion 2001, *Eighteen Turns*
Designed by Daniel Libeskind with Arup

ARoS Aarhus Kunstmuseum, Denmark; a commissioned proposal for The Hirshhorn Museum and Sculpture Garden, The Smithsonian Institution's museum of modern and contemporary art in Washington DC, which reconsiders the communicative potential of the museum; and a façade design for The Icelandic National Concert and Conference Centre in Reykjavik, due for completion in 2009. He has also been involved in a number of architectural projects with Thorsen and the team at Snøhetta, including a proposal for Turner Contemporary in Margate, 2005, and a recently submitted competition proposal for a new Museum of Contemporary Art in Warsaw. Their fascinating working process is investigated in more depth in the essays and discussion within this publication.

The Serpentine's annual architecture commission has resulted in a series of remarkable structures, and it is a challenge to the designers to sustain this high quality of architecture. And yet, without fail, our expectations are always exceeded. This year has been no exception. We must thank Olafur Eliasson and Kjetil Thorsen profusely, not only for their incredible commitment to every stage of the project, but also for conceiving such a magnificent, intelligent and dynamic structure – a landmark for London and a major contribution to the fields of contemporary art and architecture.

We are also delighted that they have worked with the Serpentine to develop *Park Nights* – the series of public events based on experimentation being held in the Pavilion throughout its life in Kensington Gardens. Building on the success of last year's programme, this year is even more ambitious, focusing on experimentation as its key theme. On Friday nights, the Pavilion will operate as a laboratory, where artists, architects, filmmakers, academics and scientists will create an environment of invention through a series of public

9

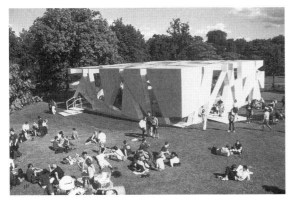

Serpentine Gallery Pavilion 2002
Designed by Toyo Ito with Arup

Serpentine Gallery Pavilion 2003
Designed by Oscar Niemeyer

experiments, screenings of experimental films and performances that will culminate in the 48-hour *Serpentine Gallery Experiment Marathon* in London and Berlin, in October and November 2007.

We also thank Eliasson and Thorsen for their contribution to this publication. We could not be more grateful to them both, for everything they have done in connection with this project.

We are indebted as well to the teams at Studio Olafur Eliasson in Berlin and Snøhetta in Oslo for their immense hard work. This dedicated design team developed the project from start to finish with energy and meticulousness. Sebastian Behmann brought his considerable experience to the project and gave important overall guidance. Ricardo Gomes indomitably devoted more time than any other person involved with the Pavilion and with zealous attention has drawn and coordinated virtually every aspect of the design. In their work, they were ably assisted by Ben Allen, Andreas Eggertsen and Aase Mortensen. Further support was given by Néstor Pérez Batista, Erik Huber, Sharron Ping Jen Lee, Andreas Nypan, Sven Pfeiffer, Joshua Teas, and Rune Veslegard. Our thanks are also extended to members of the expanded design team, brought on board by the designers for their particular specialisms: Robert Banović and Norbert Palz, Targa Design, for visualisation and production assistance; Palz also worked closely with the design team to develop the complex geometry of the seating; Fredrik Wenstøp and Kristian Wenstøp, both at Pivot, for 3-D modelling assistance; and Erik Nordbye, ebn design. We also recognise the role of Petra Rickhof who patiently and efficiently coordinated numerous aspects of the overall project. To everyone involved in this project in Berlin and Oslo, we offer our sincerest thanks.

10

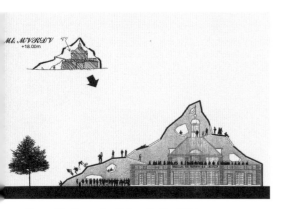

Concept for Serpentine Gallery Pavilion 2004
Designed by MVRDV with Arup

Serpentine Gallery Pavilion 2005
Designed by Álvaro Siza and Eduardo Souto de Moura
with Cecil Balmond — Arup

The structural engineering of this year's Pavilion has been skilfully developed by Dr Switbert Greiner who, supported by Jörg Beierbach, Attila Bodenseh and Herwig Bretis, worked closely with the design team to develop a structure that could be realised within the inherent restraints of the project.

Since 2001, Peter Rogers, Managing Director, Stanhope plc, has played a pivotal role in the Serpentine Gallery annual architecture commissions. His expertise in every aspect of the engineering and construction process has enabled him to advise at each stage in the development of the structure, as well as to champion the project to associates in the industry whose support has also been key to its success. That he does so with such immense expertise and good humour makes working with him a joy, and we cannot begin to express our gratitude.

Our advisors for this project on the Serpentine Gallery Board of Trustees are Lord Palumbo, Chairman, and Chairman of the Jury of the Pritzker Prize for Architecture, and Zaha Hadid, Trustee, and 2004 Pritzker Laureate. We are grateful to them and to the entire Board of Trustees for their continuing support of the annual architecture commission.

Arup has played an advisory role in this year's structure, and we are indebted first and foremost to Cecil Balmond, Deputy Chairman, for continuing to recognise the significance of these commissions and for offering Arup's resources and to Daniel Bosia, Peter Bressington, Pat Dallard, David Deighton, Anthony Ferguson, Florian Gauss, Alistair Guthrie, Martin Manning, Dorothee Richter, Becci Taylor, James Thonger, Mick White and Peter Williams.

The former Project Manager of Serpentine Gallery Pavilions from 2000 to 2006, Mark Robinson, was a Project Advisor in the initial

Serpentine Gallery Pavilion 2006
Designed by Rem Koolhaas and Cecil Balmond, with Arup

Lilas by Zaha Hadid Architects 2007
Zaha Hadid and Patrik Schumacher

stages of the project, and we are most grateful to him for sharing his invaluable knowledge and experience.

The financial support of a number of inspired companies and individuals who truly believe in the importance of this unique strand of the Serpentine's programming is key. We are delighted that, for a second year running, Bloomberg has pledged considerable financial support to the Pavilion. We offer our thanks, in particular, to Patti Harris and Bloomberg for their sustained commitment, especially Lex Fenwick and Jemma Read.

We are also indebted to the individuals who have offered their support to the project, in particular to the Serpentine Summer Circle: Honorary Patron, Novator Partners LLP; Patron, Sigurður Gísli Pálmason; Benefactors, Marianne Holtermann and Lance Entwistle; Mrs Turidur Reynisdottir; and Siri Stolt-Nielsen, as well as those who wish to remain anonymous.

The Council of the Serpentine Gallery is crucial to our success in manifold ways and our enormous thanks go to them, as well as to Richard and Ruth Rogers for their continued involvement in the Pavilion.

The success of the Pavilion is also dependent on the encourage-ment and backing of a number of key organisations.

Mark Camley, Chief Executive of the Royal Parks, together with his colleagues, Colin Buttery, Director of Parks, and Tom Jarvis, Royal Parks Manager – Kensington Gardens, have continued to recognise the significant contribution that these structures make to the Royal Park of Kensington Gardens; their advocacy of this year's scheme has been essential.

We also extend our thanks to the Friends of Hyde Park and Kensington Gardens, and in particular to the Co-Chairs, Lady Cleaver and Jacqueline Hyer, for giving the proposed scheme their blessing at an early stage.

The assistance of many people at Westminster City Council is crucial to the realisation of the architectural commission. We would like to thank, in particular, Councillor Angela Hooper, Chairman of Planning and City Development Committee, and the planning committee members, Councillors Duncan Sandys (Chairman), Susie Burbridge, Christabel Flight and Barbara Grahame, as well as Rosemarie MacQueen, Director of Planning and City Development; Gwyn Richards, Conservation and Urban Design; Charles Vaton, District Surveyor, and Jenny Wilson, District Surveyors – Licensing.

We must also recognise the role played by Roger Parncutt at the London Fire and Emergency Planning Authority in advising us on our safety strategy.

Over the years, the Serpentine Gallery Pavilion has been built using a variety of materials, and part of the process has been to find companies who are willing and able to commit considerable resources to supplying and manufacturing these elements. In 2007, the two key materials are steel and timber. Under the direction of Richard and Heinrich Rohlfing, the German company Rohlfing has shown great proficiency in the construction of the steel. The timber cladding has been efficiently produced by NÜSSLI (Switzerland) Ltd, led by Martin Joos, Head of Division, and Peter Wattinger, Project Leader.

The construction of the Pavilion would also not be possible without the kind support of a large number of companies, some of whom have supported our Pavilions in previous years and others who are new to the project. Our heart-felt gratitude is extended to all those listed below:

Bovis Lend Lease Limited, for providing project management, construction management and CDM co-ordination. We express our sincere thanks to Alexander Dietrich and Bernard Franklin for committing their time, knowledge and expertise to the realisation of the project, to Cyrus Khazai and Gary Maloney for managing the construction site, and to their colleagues Julian Daniel, Head of UK South; Paul Sims, Account Manager, and Tony McAree, Construction Director.

We are delighted to have the support of lighting experts Zumtobel for the first time and would like to thank Jürg Zumtobel and Herbert Resch, in particular.

Chris Massie, Marketing Director, Clipfine, for organising the provision of security for the Pavilion and providing a slinger/signaller on site.

Richard Baldwin and Paul Davis, Partners, and Jonathan Dixon, Project Surveyor of Davis Langdon LLP, for their role as quantity surveyors.

Barnaby Collins, Partner, DP9, for all his advice concerning planning, including our application to Westminster City Council, which went smoothly as a result.

Brendan Kerr, Managing Director, Keltbray, for offering to undertake the dismantling of the Pavilion from its site in Kensington Gardens.

Serpentine Gallery Trustee Marco Compagnoni and his colleagues, including Jonathan Wood, Samantha McGonigle and James Swan of Weil, Gotshal & Manges, for providing invaluable *pro-bono* legal advice throughout the project.

Pat Stanborough, Chief Executive, and Barry Deflaco, Managing Director, and the team at T. Clarke, including Paul Brown, Divisional Director; Russell Jones, Site Manager, and Joe Whipp, Contracts Manager for the electrical installation.

Keith Duncan, Design Manager, and Alan Collen, Construction Manager, Barr Construction, for supplying and fitting the timber seating that is so integral to the design of the building.

Simon Benton, Director, and his team at The Bradley Collection, for providing fixtures for the curtains and assisting in their installation.

Pat Carey, Civil Engineering Operations Director, and Ambikapathy Aravinthan, Contracts Manager at Carey Group PLC, for contributing an excavation driver and undertaking landscaping works at the emergency exit.

Ian Dunbar, Manager, EMS, for providing temporary power and water.

Kevin Richardson and Kevin Burrows, Directors, and Russell Chandler, Project Manager, Gardner & Co, for supplying ducting for the integrated heating system.

David Hodgkiss, Chief Executive, and Nick Day, Director, and their teams at William Hare Ltd, for their contribution in the early stages of the project and for co-ordinating Debbie McCarthy, Commercial Manager, Safety Net Services to provide the internal safety netting during the construction period.

Stef Stefanou, Chairman, and John Storey, Contracts Manager, and their colleagues at John Doyle Group, for once again completing the excavation and concreting necessary for the foundations, as well as providing site welfare facilities.

Maximilian Rebensburg, Konzept:werk, for the manufacture of the façade elements.

Anders Byriel and Henrik Kjerrumgaard at Danish textile company Kvadrat, for supplying the curtains and ball seating.

Stuart Ross, Director, and Dave Burke, Contracts Manager, Lyndon Scaffolding Plc, for offering scaffolding and a rain cover to allow work to continue on site in wet weather.

John Mann, Director, and Colin Jacob, Designer, Protec, for supplying the fire alarm.

Light test at Studio Olafur Eliasson, 2004

Gavin Perry and John Gaffney, SES, for surveying and setting out the site.

Mark Herlihy, Commercial Manager, and the team at Select Plant Hire Co Ltd – Cranes, for providing cranes and site equipment necessary for the erection of the Pavilion and for co-ordinating his colleagues Lee-Anne Bennett, Sales Manager, Nationwide, for the hire of, and training for, access equipment and Robert Bird, Director, Ladybird Crane Hire, for the hire of, and training for, the tower crane.

Gary Saunders, Managing Director; Perry Chimes, Project Coordinator; Steve Moore, Designer, and their colleagues at Swift Horsman Ltd for the construction of the café/bar.

John Massey, Director, and the team at Vector Foiltec, for fabricating and fitting the rooflight.

Bob Dempsey, Manager, Wilson James, for transportation in London and Christian Labhardt, Business Unit Manager, TSK General Transport, for transportation from Switzerland.

Mark Best, Contracts Manager, CMF, for providing and painting the handrail.

Beyond the construction of the structure, there are other companies and individuals who have contributed to this project. We are delighted to have *The Guardian* as media partner of the Serpentine Gallery Pavilion 2007. The promotion of the building and the associated events programme, both in the newspaper and online, bring our project to a wider audience. Our thanks in particular go to Alan Rusbridger, Editor; Marc Sands, Marketing Director; Sara Rhodes, Head of Sponsorship and Events, and Vanessa Smith, Sponsorship and Events Executive.

The *Park Nights* programme benefited from a magnificent group of advisors: John Brockman, Jean Max Colard, Tim Etchells, Adrian Heathfield, Luc Steels and Israel Rosenfeld and we are also indebted to Francesca von Habsburg and Daniela Zyman of T-B A21 Thyssen-Bornemisza Art Contemporary.

The programme is has been made possible by The Annenberg Foundation and we are especially grateful to Liz Kabler for her enthusiasm and support. We also extend our thanks to the Royal Norwegian Embassy, London, and The Royal Commission for the Exhibition of 1851 Foundation for their generosity, and to the Embassy of Denmark, London, for their kind assistance.

We would like to acknowledge Ran Avidan, Managing Director, and his team at GAIL's for providing the café for this year's Pavilion.

We are proud to publish this catalogue to accompany this year's architecture commission. Our thanks go to Ilka and Andreas Ruby and to Doreen Massey for their interesting and insightful texts.

The development of this publication was expertly overseen by Caroline Eggel and Anna Engberg-Pedersen, Art Historians at Studio Olafur Eliasson. Engberg-Pedersen also worked closely with the Serpentine team on the public relations and the *Park Nights* programme.

This handsome book has been designed by Michael Heimann and Hendrik Schwantes with photography by Ludwig Abache and Luke Hayes and by Anna Sofie Hartmann, Studio Olafur Eliasson. It benefited from the editorial expertise of Melissa Larner and we are pleased to be collaborating with the eminent producer of architectural books, Lars Müller Publishers.

The Serpentine's Head of Buildings and Operations, Julie Burnell, has taken over the reins as Project Leader and this year's Pavilion would not have been possible without her indefatigable dedication. Rebecca Morrill has been this year's Project Organiser and the *Park Nights* series has been brought together by Sally Tallant, Head of Education and Public Programmes, with Emma Ridgway, Public Programmes Organiser assisted by the *Experiment Marathon: London* Organisers, Richard Birkett, Cathy Haynes and Kate Stancliffe. The project has also particularly benefited from the energies of Fern Stoner, Head of Finance, and Louise McKinney, Head of Development, as well as the whole Serpentine team.

To all the many people mentioned here, as well as those not named, but who have also played a role, our appreciation could not be greater.

Julia Peyton-Jones
Director, Serpentine Gallery and Co-Director, Exhibitions & Programmes

Hans Ulrich Obrist
Co-Director, Exhibitions & Programmes and Director, International Projects

LARS
KÜNSTLER

ARNE
NÆSS

ARCHICEUTICAL
&
WATER

FUNCTIONAL
FOOD

KALLE MIKKELBORG

JAZZ

MARATHON
48 HOURS

SERPENTINE

PARK
ENVIRO
PHILOSOP

Over

under

Olafur Eliasson and Kjetil Thorsen in Conversation with Julia Peyton-Jones and Hans Ulrich Obrist

JP-J   Can we start by talking a little bit about your working processes in collaborating on this project?

KT   One of the things we've been discussing when it comes to our working processes is the difference between the analogue and the digital process. On an old-fashioned type-writer, for instance, you have to know the full sentence before you can start typing it because it would be too much work to start all over again each time you changed your mind. So you sketch the whole piece of writing out before you commit it to print. The digital process means that you don't have to know the end result: you can change things during the process. Then it's just a matter of creating the environment for that process, which at that point has an uncertain goal within an uncertain time frame. Using digital tools, you can change positions: departing from point A with an uncertain result at point B. This is what the process has been about so far.

HUO   This relationship between analogue and digital is very interesting. Some years ago, the artist Gustav Metzger raised the question of the disappearance of analogue drawing because of digital tools.

OE   To me, the important thing is that Kjetil and I have the same approach in terms of content. When I say 'content', I don't mean a programmatic sense of content; I mean intentionality, and a kind of free trajectory: not knowing exactly where it's heading. We wouldn't start out by drawing a curved line, for example, and then talk about what that could be used for. Normally we'd approach it the other way around, by saying, 'We have a desire, we have a dream, we have intentions and we want to execute them', and for that we need to have a form — we need some degree of containment in order to sustain the values we believe in. Then we would ask, 'What does the line look like?'

It was after building that sense of a common trajectory through discussion that we started talking about drawing. This is how the idea of the spiral came about: using temporality as a very instrumental part of the Pavilion, looking at the previous Pavilions and trying to leave what has already been done behind and to add new layers of meaning to it. In the

19

beginning we'd normally use analogue tools – drawing with pens – but I don't think it's very interesting to ask whether one draws with analogue or digital means. There's a tendency to romanticise 'Meister' drawings – and I guess in some cases it's justified – but if you're good at both types of drawings, there's no clear difference between analogue and digital. For me, it's about practicalities and about speed. Digital drawing is extremely slow, but it does save time at the other end, when you have to calculate how many square metres you need. Analogue drawing is very fast in the beginning but slow at the end. So you start with analogue drawing and use the digital tools later. It's as pragmatic as that.

KT   Drawing is a way of thinking. It's a conceptual rather than a diagrammatic way of explaining, of clarifying. To me, the relationship between drawing and thinking is not limited to the specific tool of communication. The drawing is worth more than its value as artistic expression, although diagrams can be fantastically beautiful, and to transform that drawing into a digital production is just a different part of the process. The pencil and the computer are only tools; they're not as important as the people behind them,

but in any case they're similar; they're just different parts of the process.

HUO   Did you do the drawings together or did one of you make them and the other one edit them? Does it work a little bit like a palimpsest?

KT   When you're talking about your ideas in a workshop situation, analogue drawing is an essential tool. You could call it Mischkunst – the mixing of arts. It's like a game where you make one drawing, then the next person takes that drawing and copies it, almost, but adds a different angle, and thus it develops into a consensual understanding of what you're trying to achieve.

JP-J   Could you talk about how you conceived the project in relation to London, and not only London, but the park in which we sit, which is both part of the city and separate from the city. Was that factored into your ideas at all?

OE   Yes. A city, with all its history, reflects the value systems at the time when its neighbourhoods were developed, and urban planning reveals the dominant ideologies. And the same goes for the park: it's a wonderful recreational area within the city, and it's also a construction of nature, an exhibition of a certain idea of life. And here we have

20

a teahouse, the Serpentine, which has since become a gallery. When the teahouse was built, the aristocratic, oriental fashion of having tea while enjoying nature was at its peak. It was a highly constructed situation and therefore not about reality; it was about the construction of reality. Nowadays, the teahouse is used for exhibitions that are also not reality, but pictures of reality, which then, as a consequence, become reality. On top of that, there's the tradition of making Pavilions, which in a sense are not real buildings. It's a display-oriented trajectory, from the large exhibitions in the 19th century to modern ones like the Frieze Art Fair. So, throughout the history of the relationship between the park and the city, between the Serpentine and the park and between the Serpentine and the Pavilion, we see an ongoing negotiation of what constitutes reality. This determines the degree to which we allow people to understand the potential of this construction as a means to re-evaluate themselves in relation to their surroundings.

The Pavilion is different from an urban house: it has a distinct relationship with a constructed natural setting, like follies in French and English gardens. Also like the folly, it aims to be unpredictable. So here

we have a set of rules, or a tradition at least, where the idea is to be unpredictable; the Pavilion must perform something different from an urban house in a street in the city of London. The reflexive potential of such a structure, the question of what type of performativity is built into this complex event, is what we had to sit down and talk about before we could actually get to the point of designing and drawing. This is why every aspect of the Pavilion also makes reference to the other parts of it. There's no vanishing point; there's no ending – well, there is an ending, but it's ...

KT   A re-routing.

OE   It's not a goal in itself; it's just a construction and you have to go back down the ramp to leave the building.

KT   The contemporary understanding of what generates urbanism tends to overrate certain factors, like, for instance, a critical mass of people, or defined spaces enclosed with walls that generate the outdoor coordinates of a structure. The Pavilion is sited in an urban-park context, so it's defined by the urban setting – not by being within a typology or outside a typology; it's born in that real situation. With an urban building like a church, you have a freestanding structure within

a very tight urban situation. Of course, there's a more important side and a less important side to a church, but there isn't a back side as there is with a house. And this is also true of the Pavilion. So to me, that means that it can't be expanded, it can't grow, it can't be higher or lower; it is what it is. Its form is not related directly to symmetry, nor to the typology of the structure, but to our early investigations into geometric sequences and to the setting in which the object is born. Having been born in Norway, for example, I can't claim that I'm not Norwegian just because I have a different passport, but I might not be typical as a result of that. So you create realities that are defined by the realities around you.

HUO   Olafur mentioned the folly, which Cedric Price defined as a distortion of space and time. There's also the tradition of the grotto in the 18th-century English garden. This links to last year's programme, when we had Thomas Demand's work *Grotto* in the Gallery. Lately, architecture has become obsessed with icons like Frank Gehry's Guggenheim Museum in Bilbao that concentrate on exterior complexity, as opposed to forms such as the 18th-century grotto that opt for interior complexity. Can you talk a little bit about this idea of interior complexity? The Pavilion becomes pretty dense inside, in terms of the way the seating works in an almost organic way.

OE   The Bilbao-effect was very much a phenomenon of the 1990s. I think we're now moving out of the Bilbao era, but maybe Dubai, by simply duplicating the world Las Vegas-style, will create another such effect. Instead, we're witnessing the trends of experience economy and event management that often separate form from content. I think I can say for both of us that we don't reject form, since it is of course still very productive, but today we find so many icons that all take away the performative aspect of objects. In general a lot of icons are being built all over the world that don't actually achieve anything; they don't perform, except as desirable objects in marketing terms. With our Pavilion we're attempting to re-establish a degree of performativity.

KT   Actually, I think the iconic started with Jørn Utzon's Opera House in Sydney.

OE   You could even say it goes back to the Eiffel Tower.

KT   These iconic works represent an undefined need in society: they're just snap-shots of certain conditions that are generated by a lack of something else. Very often,

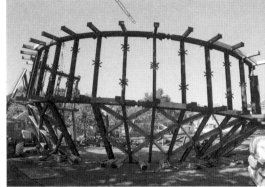

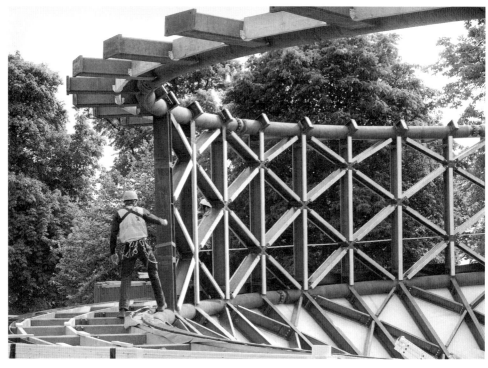

architecture is formalised by the lack of something. That's why they'll cease to be built: they're not fulfilling anything.

A grotto, on the other hand, has a sheltering aspect; it romanticises the idea of shelter and intimacy. The space is defined by the human physical condition – standing, sitting, lying, whatever the body's condition might be in that sheltering situation. In the dwellings of the Lepenski Vir, built between 6400 and 4600 BC in what is now Serbia, you move sideways when entering, because the intention is that you can't look into the space before you enter it. To some extent, the romantic experience of the cave is related to its missing front wall, which generates the space behind; it's like a tunnel. There's the sense that you're penetrating the surface. And if you generate an artificial cave, you generate more air space on earth than you had before because you're expanding the surface of the earth in square metres. You've taken away a mass of earth and put it somewhere else, or thrown it into the ocean. The intimacy of the space is connected to the fact that you're capturing air space that's common property and putting it into a defined area so that the air you breathe inside there belongs to you. And all the senses you use in these interior spaces are related to why you feel safe in a cave, even though there might not be enough light, and there might be something hiding round the next corner, so there's also a dangerous feeling related to it. That's the challenging aspect of the grotto.

OE   One of the things that have interested me on the few occasions I've explored Icelandic grottos was the difference between that particular experience and the negotiation of a perpendicularly organised environment such as a cube-shaped house. In a grotto, because you have to climb and crawl and slide through tiny holes and work your way in through the innards, there's no information telling you what's up and what's down. Going into a grotto makes you feel very heavy because you're going closer to the centre of the earth, and you have the kind of feeling of suspense that you experience in an empty swimming pool where there's no water but you can still almost feel it. On the other hand, due to constantly having to organise what's up and what's down and what's far and what's near, you lose track of gravity and you start to feel as if you're floating. It's not that you lose yourself, but the need for recomposing yourself becomes obvious.

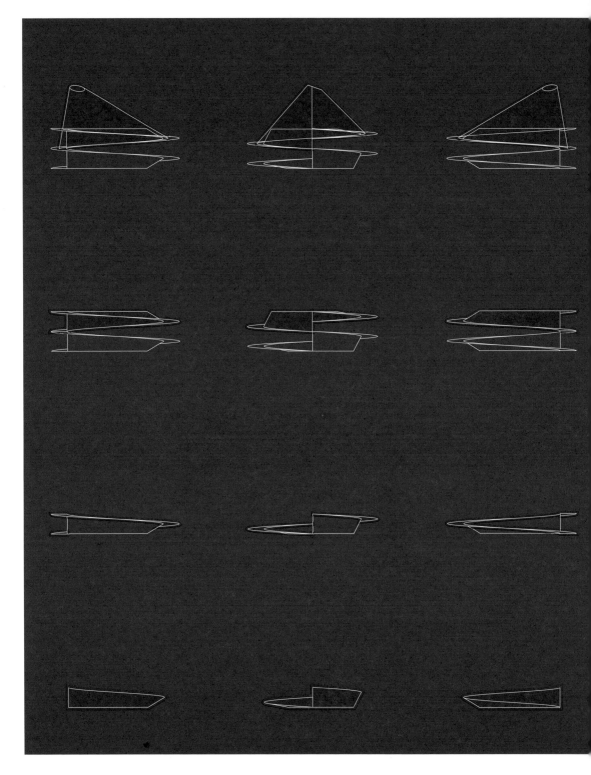

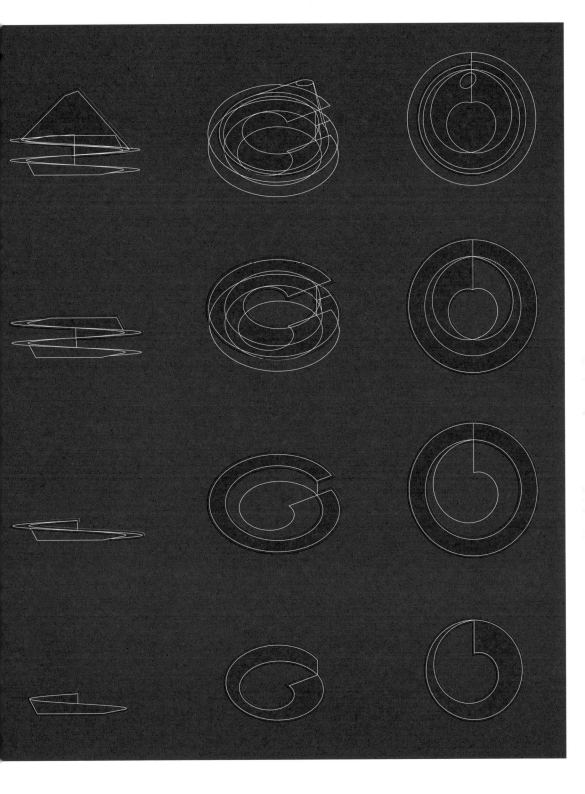

KT   If you go to the cave dwellings at Petra in Jordan, where there's a certain amount of getting under the skin of the surfaces, it's like being born again. As you move in and out of the caves, it's as if you're being continuously reborn. I think there is this rebirth issue with the cave, like being in the womb, which also has to do with the weightlessness that Olafur was describing.

OE   The border of yourself is no longer your skin, but the space in which you are; you start to attach and define yourself based on the skin of the space. The Pavilion did have, earlier in the design process, a grotto period. There was a time when the cone of the roof was extremely animated.

KT   And we did have that discussion about turning things upside down, but I'm happy it became more about the simplified function of the space rather than a complex relationship to a grotto kind of condition.

OE   I agree.

JP-J   Why did you choose wood for the skin of the Pavilion, and why that particular colour?

OE   It had to do both with practicalities and our desire to create a sensitive relationship between our vision and accessible materials. There's something very liberating about wood, in that it can easily change form. The tendency has been to imply a certain degree of built-in, essentialist qualities in wood, which I'm very sceptical about, and this is why we've stressed the rather industrial feeling of the wood in the Pavilion — to avoid ascribing fixed, universal qualities to it. I think the reason for this tendency is that wood has been ascribed a kind of aura, which has resulted in many designers choosing to use something less stigmatised such as plastic materials. It was our intention to show that wood can in fact be very organic and pleasant and productive to have around; it has a great sense of performativity.

KT   I think the reason why wood has been stigmatised is because within the development of Scandinavian architecture, and of modern architecture in general, it has been seen as private, while brick is related to the public sphere. Because of this, and because of its organic nature, until the late 1980s one wouldn't have believed it possible to build public buildings using wood. We made a huge mistake as a society in believing that public buildings are non-tactile. The public sphere is just as tactile as the private, and you have to be just as precise about the expectations of the general public as about

29

those of an individual. The qualities of appearance have no basic differences when it comes to practicality. So to me, wood has all the advantages already mentioned: it can be industrialised, it's extremely environmentally friendly if used correctly without destroying the rainforest, and it has all the qualities that you want from an organic material. These qualities just need to be enhanced through a tactile relationship between materials, people and objects.

HUO   One of the ways in which you do that is through the form of the building, which has a spiralling dynamic. I recently spoke to the young architects Aranda and Lasch in New York, who said that the spiral is a shape unlike any other because it's seldom experienced as geometry but rather as energy. I found this very interesting in relation to your building.

OE   When talking about spirals and geometry, I believe one has to think in terms of the people in the space. The way in which we've organised the spiralling form is less about the form for its own sake, and more about how people move within the space. The building has the form it has because this supports a certain way of moving. The unusual thing is, the closer to the edge of the building

you go, the faster you move; the further out on the ramp you are, the more you move. In the centre, you're more likely to stand still. If you think of another kind of space, like an Italian piazza, people sit around the edge, and in the middle they tend to zig-zag. We've reversed that in order to sustain a field in the centre with a very high degree of focus. There's also the idea of the cone as a spinning top, where the point that moves the least is where it touches the ground. The spiralling movement creates a means of focusing: people on the ramp will understand that they're looking into the space but also being looked at from this space where people tend not to move. There's something to this idea of drawing people towards the centre, just as a vortex or funnel takes things and pulls them towards the centre, in terms of generating a momentum or a participatory relationship with the Pavilion. You feel you're a part of something: you're not just passing by. The intention is to show that indifference is not very productive, and that difference, instead of being a segregational way of organising a space, can become an asset and an element producing the space. Different speeds, different kinds of movement, different ideas and types

of coming together, can actually constitute a sense of collectivity.

What's unique about this park is that you feel alone when you walk through it, yet if you really were the only one in the park, it would be very strange and uncomfortable. It's an odd situation where you need a sense of the collective in order to be alone, an idea of the singular/plural. In my view, some of the other Pavilions have been less concerned with the need to address the fact that you're a single person but you're also part of a social event. The question is how to sustain a tolerant frame where you can acknowledge the differences between people and use this actively. This is why the production of reality is not about reality per se, it's about democracy being concerned with difference rather than with sameness. So the idea of the spiralling movement — forces, geometry, sequences in space — all fit round these beliefs and values about social relationships.

KT   I like the thought that you can separate energy from geometry, but in essence everything that grows, grows around the spiral. In the transformative process of growth, through energy pulled from the earth or the air, the growth pattern of any plant or organic material is based on the 5-, 7-, 9-, 11-edged

spiral. You see it clearly in the cactus, for instance, but every little blade of grass out there is a spiral. This relates to the way in which water runs down the plughole, gravity and so forth. So energy and geometry are strongly related. In the Pavilion, you don't move directly from one position to the other as you walk along the ramp; you go in two directions: you go up and you go round, and that again is to do with the complexity of the social situation rather than the simple organic extraction of energy and growth.

JP-J   Your Pavilion really encapsulates the idea of the promenade. It's about the counterpoint between the exterior and the interior, but also about how the park is used by people displaying themselves to each other. This idea of being seen is more of a Continental European phenomenon than a British one, isn't it?

KT   In Margate you get that European sense along the seafront, the promenade. But I think it's extremely important that you can meet people face to face while passing each other. That's the whole issue about promenading, although Laurie Anderson said that walking is simply preventing yourself from falling forwards! So if you have a sense of promenading in this Pavilion, it isn't so

33

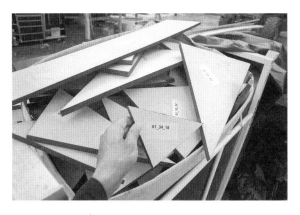

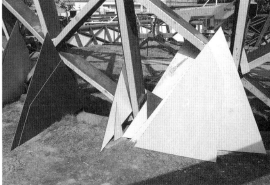

much about walking, as about walking past someone, face to face.

OE   There aren't many places in society today where the journey is seen as part of whatever experience you are having. Experiences have more or less been taken over by the experience economy. In museology or the ideology involved in the communication of art, the journey and the promenade are never really given the prominence they deserve. The museum is a place that's highly regulated, and very much about power. But the promenade is interesting in the sense that it's a temporal phenomenon. Nobody would think of reducing the promenade to just the moment, when you see a seagull flying past, for instance. There's an interesting book by Rebecca Solnit [*Wanderlust: A History of Walking*] on this idea of the promenade and walking in general. It looks at the European tradition of the *flâneur* and continues to the museum and shopping malls. Promenades are sometimes mistakenly understood as being paths in nature, but many are organised around the city's defence systems: the waterfront or the walk from one tower of the city wall to the next. The Royal Parks and Kensington Gardens don't have an English garden layout, but if you go down to the other end of Hyde Park, it's more organic and more of a typical English garden. The reason why it's axial closer to the Palace is because this makes it easier to control the park. You can shoot with a rifle down a straight path without the bullet being deflected. So the promenade is also about safety, about guarding the social structure. In the Austrian-Swiss mountains, when they built the fortresses against the Italians, the best vantage point for the castle was where you would see the valley. This would also be the most picturesque point, so there you have military strategy overlapping with the idea of the beautiful view.

JP-J   Clearly, the relationship of the Pavilion to the park is important to you, but what about the relationship of the Pavilion to the Gallery building? Álvaro Siza, for example, described his Pavilion as like a crouching animal ready to pounce on the Gallery. Could your Pavilion be described with a similar sort of simile?

KT   It's already been done: the spinning top.

OE   I don't think there's a formal relationship in terms of the shape, the materials, the size, but there's no way around the fact that the Pavilion is connected to the Serpentine building. Being a teahouse, the Gallery itself

34

originated from the idea of a Pavilion for recreational activities, so there's a relationship right there. And then there's the simple fact that they're located next to each other. I've always thought of the front lawn of the Serpentine as being like a porch or a kind of pedestal. It's as if you're in the park, but not really. Due to the history of the other Pavilions, that particular space is no longer just the park, but the Pavilion spot and that's why the Serpentine has a strong relationship with it. One shouldn't underestimate the representational power of the previous Pavilions. There are so many expectations in that particular footprint and we need to take into consideration how we avoid the ephemera being lost along the way. If we insist on ephemera being important for philosophical and social reasons, how do we avoid that spot in front of the Serpentine ruling out ephemera in favour of the spectacle? I experienced the same challenge with *The weather project* for Tate Modern's Turbine Hall, because it was sometimes described simply as 'the sun' and almost became an icon in itself. We don't want either extreme; we want to balance it responsibly. We want it to be a significant form but we also want it to produce ephemera and reality. The first Pavilion probably didn't have the same need to stress the temporality because it was already there.

JP-J   It was built in.

OE   It was already on the site. But now the site has become a plinth, a pedestal, and slowly the feeling of time has changed or disintegrated, due to the politics of display. We now need to reconsider the display in order to reactivate the silent front of the Serpentine. And that's not better or worse than the situation for the previous Pavilions; it's just changing the rules of the game.

KT   That's very true. In deciphering or decoding the place, it's no longer a question of, 'Have you seen that Pavilion next to the Serpentine?', but, 'Have you seen this year's Pavilion?' That's a big change. So on the one hand we have to be very direct; on the other hand, in order not to lose the ephemera, we have to be indirect. If all the contexts we've been through during this process were reduced to one selling point or a nickname, I think it would lose something. But on the other hand, all the other buildings have nick-names, and maybe it's only when you love something that you give it a nickname.

HUO   The programme will also play a role in the content of the Pavilion. Could you talk

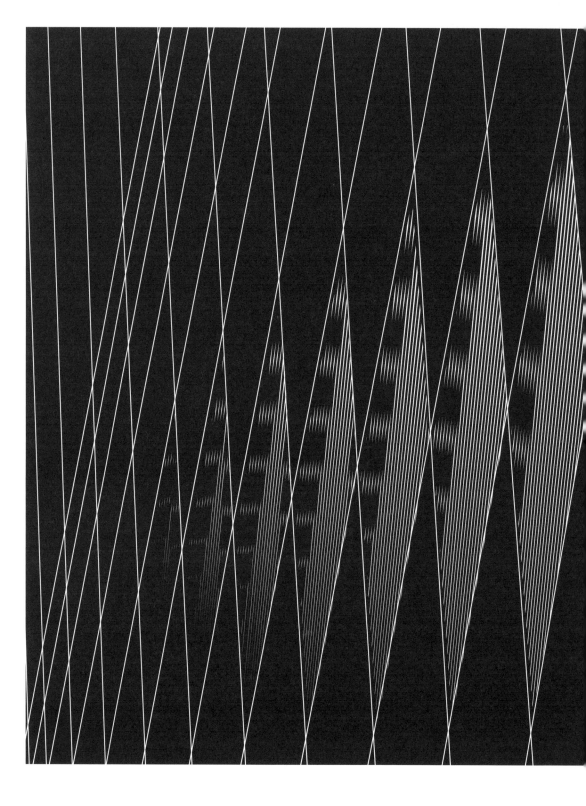

a little bit about this aspect, and about the idea of eating and drinking in the Pavilion.

OE   The third leg in the design process was a sensitivity to the public programme that will take place in and somehow respond well to the Pavilion. Since the whole idea of temporality was so instrumental to the layout of the Pavilion, we though it might be interesting to investigate how the body, as a time-based renewable source, is also a Pavilion of sorts. Every cell in our body renews itself regularly throughout our life; when we're old our body is not the same as the one we had when we were middle-aged and when we were children. I've also become increasingly interested in the structure of our senses and how we take in our surroundings, so it was a logical step to think about the mouth in terms of what things taste like. In the world of eating there's an architecture as well – the architecture of taste.

Having thought of this, I started thinking about cyclical patterns in different locations on the planet. If you're in the north, you have a dark winter and a very bright summer, which creates a special digestive system and affects the amount of chemicals being produced by the body. There's great potential for a programme event based on this.

It would be a good opportunity to collaborate with a chef on some kind of artwork in which the journey is the meal. It would not just be about the moment when we taste something, which is the typical market-orientated way of seeing food. The journey starts the moment the seed is planted in the ground outside in the park, then we carry it in, cook it, and ask what it does to our body, how it reacts, how it's influenced, how the food leaves our body through sweat and excrement.

KT   It would be fantastic to put on programmes that are related to food, and to the global discussion about the availability of water.

HUO   To finish, could we move to the question of historical precedents. Who have been your heroes or your oxygen or inspiration? Olafur has won the Kiesler Prize, and you both have an interest in Frederick Kiesler, particularly in relation to the spiral. It would be interesting to talk a little bit about that.

OE   One of the most interesting things about Kiesler was that he managed to establish a body of work and a language around it that was completely inclusive and distinct. And yet as an architect and an artist he was never quite successful; it didn't really

work as art and it didn't really work as architecture. Normally that would have meant that he wouldn't have been successful in creating a language, but he was. I think he's one of the people who has proved the increasingly important point that there's a spatial performativity out there somewhere between art and architecture that has great potential. He understood that events don't take place in a neutral environment. He was also very interested in the idea of time, and knew that the time it takes to really see something is crucial to what is actually seen. This led to his creation of the exhibition display system *Leger und Trager,* which was a way of hanging paintings off the wall. He investigated the idea of time in his *Endless House,* from 1960, which Ben van Berkel then took up in his *Möbius House.* The idea of endlessness in this work was always interpreted as if it were about an externalised idea of time, in the sense that it would take a long time to understand the house. But it was a typical modern mistake to externalise endlessness and turn it into a dogma. In my view, Kiesler's relationship with endlessness is about internal time, because you have an infinite number of relationships with that house. We also try to emphasise that with the Pavilion: we're not attempting to make a picture of time; we're trying to be of time.

KT   Yes, very nice. The only infinite space is inside you.

40

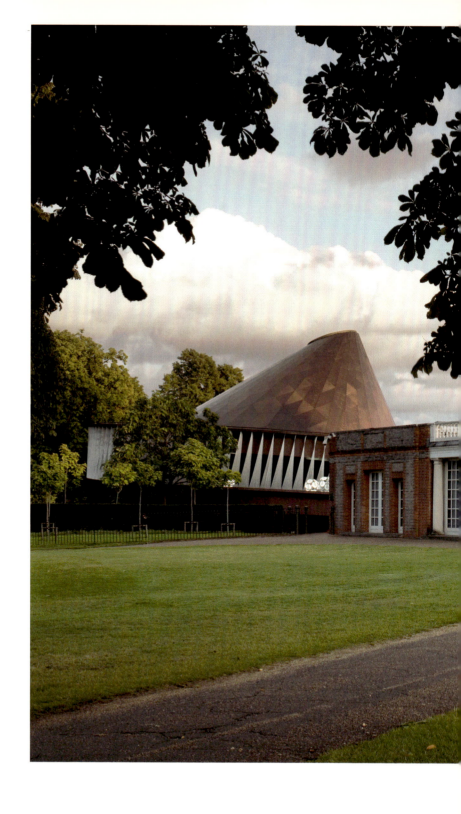

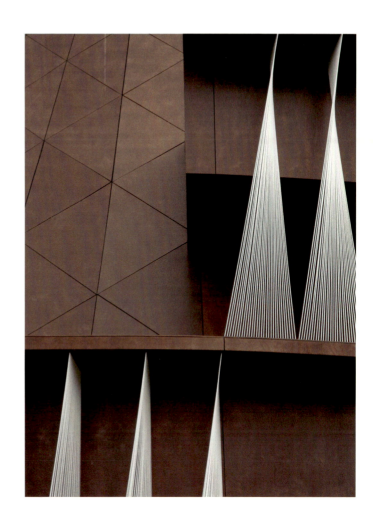

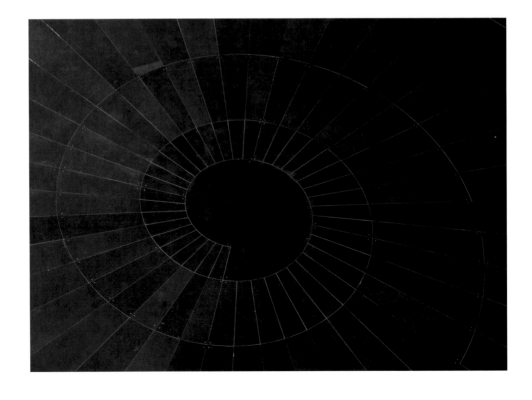

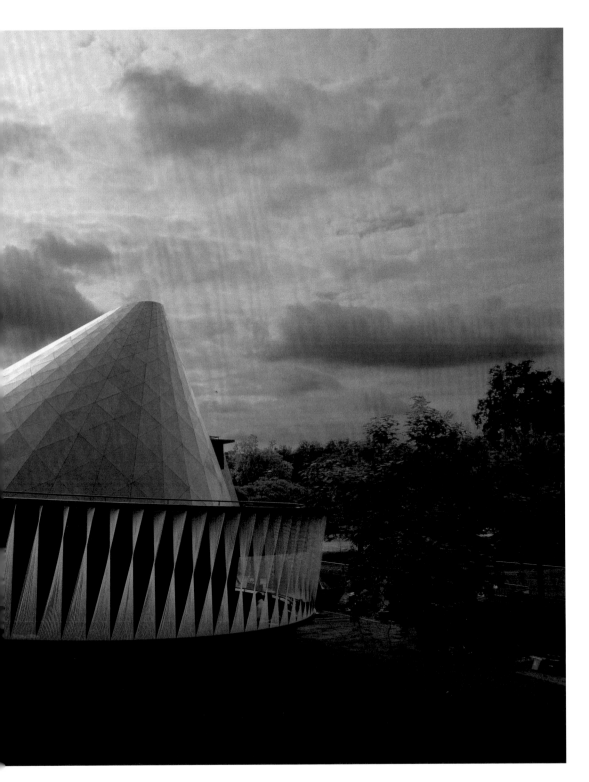

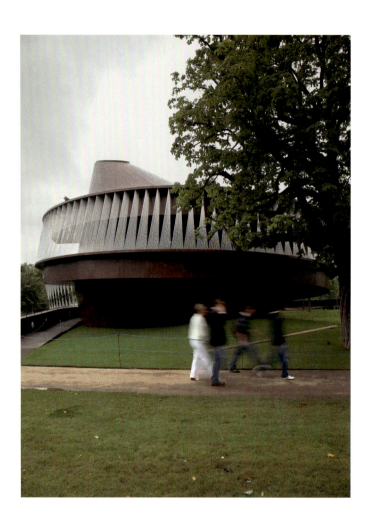

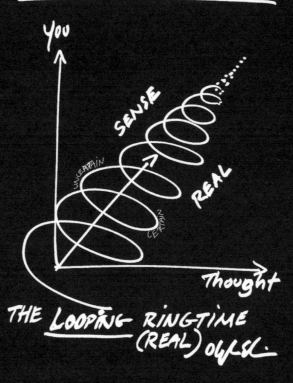

EXPECTATION FORMULA / 2006

THE <u>LOOPING</u> RINGTIME
(REAL) Olfsh.

The Mutuality of Movement

Doreen Massey

We sat in a café, above the shoreline, at St Bees in Cumbria
and looked down on the changing negotiation between sea and land.
The tide was coming in, but was being held back by a shallow
sandbar, no more than a slight swelling of the beach. Every now and
then a wave would nearly make it over the bar, then fall back,
somehow defeated. Eventually, there was enough energy and enough
sea; it breached the swelling of sand and flooded through to fill the
hollow beyond.

I watched it as a kind of struggle. The sea seemed to be *trying,*
each wave another attempt (one more push) in its negotiation with
the land. It seemed like a triumph when it made it, as though
the effort had been worthwhile (though in an hour or so it would
retreat again ...).

It was the moon and sun, of course (the former at that moment out
of sight), that were pulling the sea, giving it that energy, held in that
balance of forces of gravity in a trade-off between mass and distance.
The moon, smaller but so much nearer, is the principal force, but
as the sun and moon swing differentially in relation to each other, so
the range of the tide regularly changes. And the strength of these
forces is such that there are tides not only in the seas but also in the
so-solid earth – every day the interior of the North American continent
rises and falls by about 20 cm.[1] The very shape of the earth responds to
its position and its neighbours. When Olafur Eliasson and
Kjetil Thorsen bid us up the curling ramp, around and in and out of
their Pavilion, they are asking us to engage, in a little, personal way,
with this stupendous force.

Among the thought-experiments in what has been called 'spatial
science', one classic approach to a whole range of social issues
has been that of 'the gravity model'.[2] It has been applied to questions
of migration: the model assumes that the amount of migration
depends positively upon the problems at the point of departure and the
attractions at the other end, and inversely upon the distance to be
crossed. It has been applied to shopping: whether or not you set out is

1   I Gilmour, I Wright and J Wright, eds., *Origins of Earth and Life* (Milton Keynes:
    The Open University, 1997)
2   Spatial science is not the same as 'geography', but tends to the more quantified and
    also towards attempting to unearth universal rules. Also note that the account here
    is extremely simplified

said to depend on a trade-off between what is on offer and how far you have to go to get it. In all these models, distance (and the intervening physical world) is reduced to something to be overcome. It is an understanding of the world captured in the term 'the friction of distance'. And it is a characteristic of our times (certainly in their modern urbanised version) to apply that understanding more generally.

Distance, from this perspective, is a problem. Space, and even the physicalities of material geography, in this view, are always a burden. The point is to cross them as quickly as possible. The extollers of the age of speed-up rejoice in the death of distance; the notions of 'friction-free capitalism' and of the triumph of overcoming 'the limitations of geography' have become generalised. It is not, in fact, true as a description; it is not even possible. What is interesting is the *desire* that this ambition evinces, and also the *lack of desire* – the lack of desire for the pleasures of movement and travel; the lack of acknowledgement of the importance of the journey itself, and not just of the arrival.

For Eliasson and Thorsen, this is a slow Pavilion. It lets space take time.[3] It allows for slow travel. The slope says no to that other saying of our times: that the world is flat.

On the other hand, the notion that distance (and thus the journey) is only unwelcome friction displays a desire to transcend our earthboundness, to dematerialise into that virtual world of instantaneous communication that allows us to escape the friction of intervening encounters – precisely that element of surprise, the event of unexpected interaction, and thus the need to negotiate, that is inherent to space.

There is another aspect to spatiality and temporality here. Time/temporality is often understood as the dimension of inwardness, the dimension through which life is lived, as we experience the world, as moment succeeds moment. It is the dimension of 'becoming'. And in counterpoint there can be a certain inwardness to temporality. There is a long history of understanding subjectivity in terms of time. Space, it is in contrast sometimes assumed, is outward: not the processual experience of becoming, but the outside world within which one moves. It is pre-given, there, the landscape in which life is set. It is a counterposition that has been a persistent philosophical theme.[4]

3   And I write this as someone for whom walking can be a bit of a struggle
4   See, for instance, the account of this in Elizabeth Grosz's *Space, time and perversion: essays on the politics of bodies* (London: Routledge, 1995)

(There is a further link here, that will be picked up later, for this cosmology entails also – or can entail – that while time is the dimension of experience, space is the dimension of representation – most simply, of what we see. But hold that thought for a moment, for there are two further steps ...)

First, that the notion of time as the experience of becoming was initially centred in the individual subject: I am becoming; the rest of the world (space) is just out there. Subsequently, it dawned that if temporality was internal to one, then so it was to all; that those external things and other beings, too, were 'becoming'.[5] It is a move that brings life to space. Space becomes, then, a constantly mutating simultaneity of stories-so-far.[6] For Eliasson and Thorsen, 'temporality' is 'a constitutive element of space'.[7] Space, then, is the dimension of the social, in the sense of multiplicity, and not only the multiplicity of human stories, but the stories of rocks and stones and trees (and walls and pavilions, too). It is the dimension that presents us with the existence of others.

Second, it has also been proposed that space is the dimension of respect, and time the dimension of responsibility.[8] Space (a proper recognition of space) challenges us to a founding acknowledgement of the coeval existence of all those others, in their own temporalities. It poses, therefore, the question of how we shall respond. Time, then, is the dimension of that response.

That quotation from Eliasson and Thorsen above was not, as cited, complete. In full, it speaks of: 'temporality as a constitutive element of spaces, private or public'. Since the 1980s, we have increasingly been told (and seem widely to accept) that we are responsible for our own selves. It is seen as an element of our choice, and indeed our life-projects, our CVs, our self-absorption. We are responsible for our health in what we eat, how we exercise (and this is not incorrect, though the forces within which these 'choices' are made can thereby be hidden from view, exonerated through invisibility). We take responsibility, in other words, for our own private trajectories. And if this is true of our bodies, it is true of our finances too. Private insurance replaces mutual aid. We are individually responsible for

76

5   The story sketched here is in part a reference to Henri Bergson, a philosopher with whom Eliasson has persistently engaged

6   See Massey, D., *For Space* (London: Sage, 2005) and 'Some times of space' in Susan May, ed., Olafur Eliasson: *The weather project,* (London: Tate Publishing, 2004), pp 107–18

7   See Serpentine Gallery press release, April 2007

8   See especially Jacques Derrida, *Politics of friendship* (London: Verso, 1997)

our pensions; this is part of that fracturing of a sense of the public –
a 'public' that is precisely an acknowledgement of a wider,
mutual, responsibility – a shared responsibility for all those other,
on-going, stories. And working the exercise bike and worrying about
pensions is set within a wider powerlessness: little driven actors
of self-determination we can feel set within a wider inevitability, and
maybe indifference. 'It is as it is' in the face of the enormity of
the responsibility (even as we moan, deplore, feel guilty) for the great
spaces out there, where all those other stories are going on. This is
the difficulty of adequately acknowledging that we are, as Eliasson has
put it, 'part of a wider causality'.

Yet that distinction between inside and outside (and even, also,
between private and public) is not so clear-cut. The 'public' (even the
lack of a sense of it) is part of what constructs the 'private' individual; the outside is crucial in the constitution of the interior; the global
penetrates and is active in the production of the local. And all these
effects work the other way round too. Notions of 'setting' and
of 'context' are thus inadequate, too passive, evoking only the placing
of something in a wider location. That wider location is constitutive.
As our bodies, breathing, eating, excreting, communicating, constantly
interact with the world 'outside' – physical moments in a con-
stellation of processes – their biological rhythms (like those of many
organisms) are finely attuned to those same lunar cycles that are
part of what pulls the sea over the sand at St Bees.[9] In the same way,
this Pavilion muddles and intersects inside and out, the Pavilion
and the Park, while you climb or descend the ramp; it is one aspect of
its attempt to blur that division between, and hence the very definitions
of, outside form and content within. In the same way too, this city
itself – the quintessential local-global – is a city constructed in
a world of flows, of the migrations of people that have made it, of the
flows of capital that settle momentarily here, are controlled from here,
from the headquarters of neo-liberal globalisation. This city could
not for one moment survive, nor would its identity be in any way the
same, without all those engagements with the world beyond.

Where does this city end? What is its inside and where its outside?
'Content here includes meaning', Eliasson has said of the Pavilion.
What does this city mean? What is the effect of its trajectory in
the wider world? There are resources right now being carted across
continents to feed this place. Are the settlements and people along
their paths a part of London – drawn as they have been into the global

dynamics of the reproduction of this place? Those growing vegetables in Africa, for instance, for our tables? There is in this city not only ' the outside/the global' within, but also, if we could imagine it that way, the 'inside' beyond. That disruption of clear boundaries between inside and outside posits the possibility that, in certain realms, on certain issues, maybe it is important to imagine (aspects of) other places (those fields of green beans or of flowers) as, in a sense, part of London; and just as importantly *vice versa*, that London is 'inside' those fields of green beans and of flowers.

The strict division between inside and outside is also allied to the notion of representation. There is, in many versions of representation, a presumed exteriority. One stands apart from that which is being represented. This is one aspect of the way in which space, because of its long history of being conceived as the dimension of exteriority, of the world outside us, came to be associated with representation. And representation, in the hegemonic view, stabilises; the temporality of the trajectory is lost. The ever ongoing other stories-so-far are stabilised; the fields of flowers are pictures of fields of flowers. The stories of which they are part (germination, photosynthesis, the agroindustry, hard labour, the packing, the cellophane, the flights, the fact that they are part of us, here – and we a part of them) are stilled. It is that same distancing and lack of engagement that longs to glide through a world free of friction. This, at its most extreme, is the world as spectacle. Works of art and architecture can be extremes of this.

But this Pavilion wants to be something we *do*. It invites us over. The spiral evokes a top just asking to be spun. There is a sense of energy. Eliasson speaks of allowing 'people to understand the potential of this construction so they can use it for something them-selves in order to re-evaluate themselves in relation to their surroundings'.[10] The vortex draws you in, just as the city does. In the Turbine Hall at Tate Modern, during his *The weather project,* visitors *made* the place – it was a beach and people picnicked; it was a place of bodily experiment, and often collectively so, with people you had never met before; it was a site for a brief 'demonstration' through forming slogans in the mirror above. It was engaged with. Eliasson and Thorsen have written that 'The movement and interaction of the visitors will thus be a defining component of the Pavilion.'[11] It asks us to engage.

78

9   See Gilmour, Wright and Wright, *op. cit.*
10   See the interview in this catalogue, p 22
11   Designers' Statement, 2007

TYT 1 — A project by
Studio Olafur Eliasson

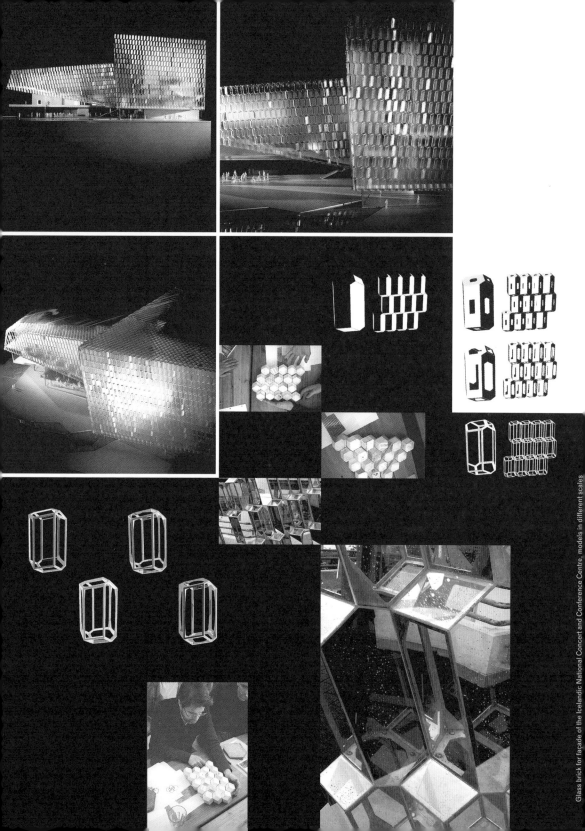

Glass brick for facade of the Icelandic National Concert and Conference Centre, models in different scales

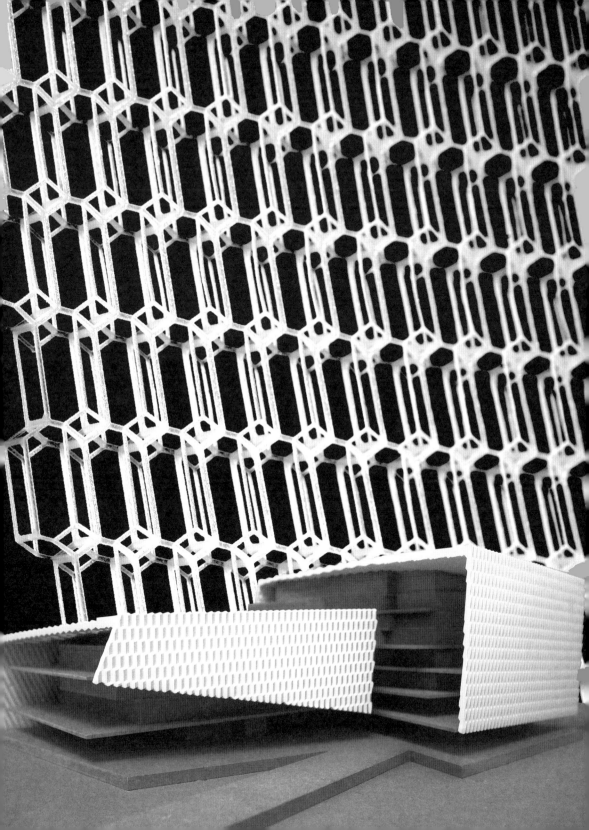

Proposal for foyer installation at
the National Opera House, Oslo, Norway

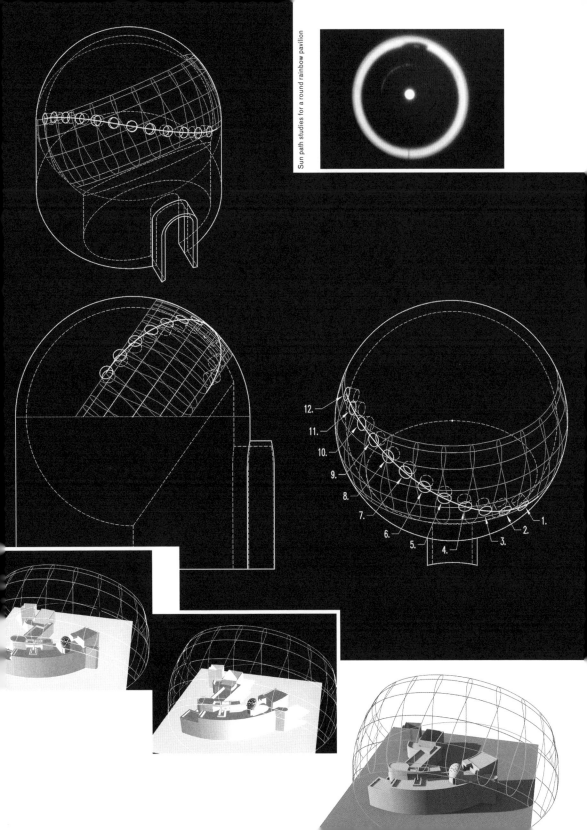

12.
11.
10.
9.
8.
7.
6.
5.
4.
3.
2.
1.

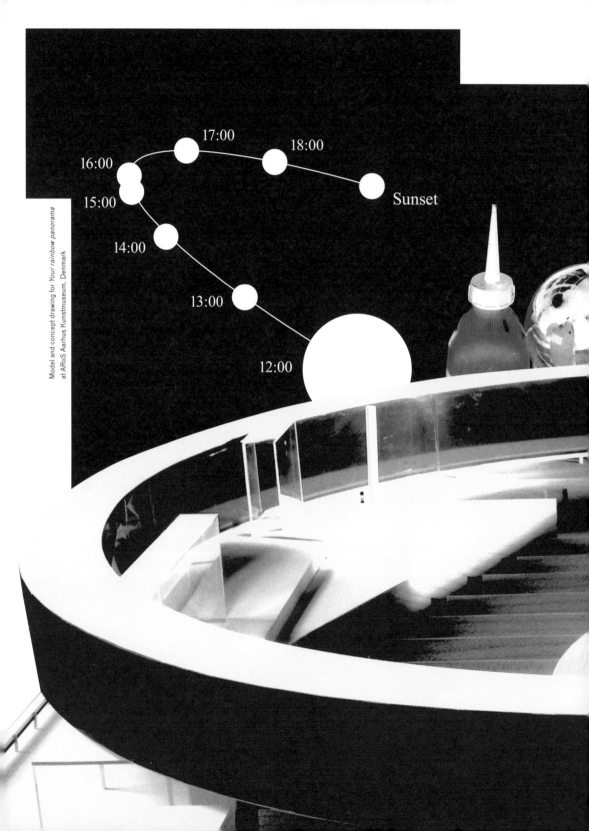

16:00

17:00

18:00

15:00

Sunset

14:00

13:00

12:00

Model and concept drawing for *Your rainbow panorama* at ARoS Aarhus Kunstmuseum, Denmark

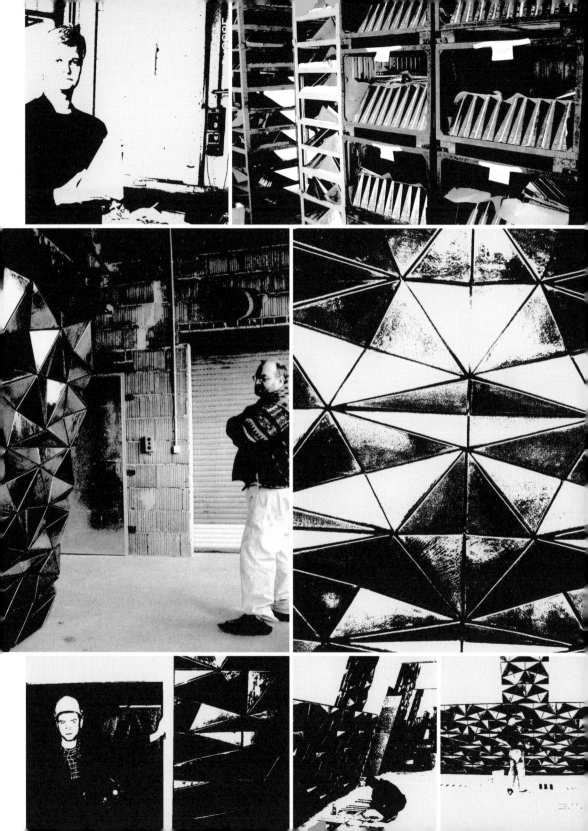

Studies for *To lufthuller med lys*
(Two air pockets with light)
for Kolding Library, Denmark

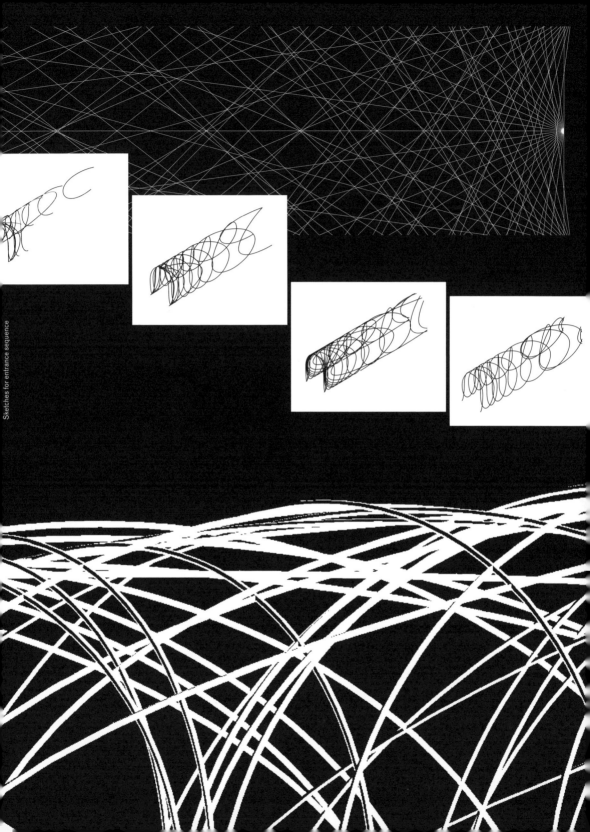

Pavés concentriques

Tile for Yu-un, 2006

The pages in this section derive from TYT magazine [Take Your Time], an ongoing project at Studio Olafur Eliasson, Berlin, begun in 2007. Its aim is to organise the current Studio research and present it to a broader audience in a magazine format, while maintaining a strong focus on the process of testing ideas and the actual development of projects and artworks. The featured works, all located in the interstices between art and architecture, investigate, in one way or another, the notion of temporality and different ways of producing space, both key considerations in Eliasson and Thorsen's development of the ramp for the Serpentine Gallery Pavilion 2007.

Studies for *Dream house*, 2007

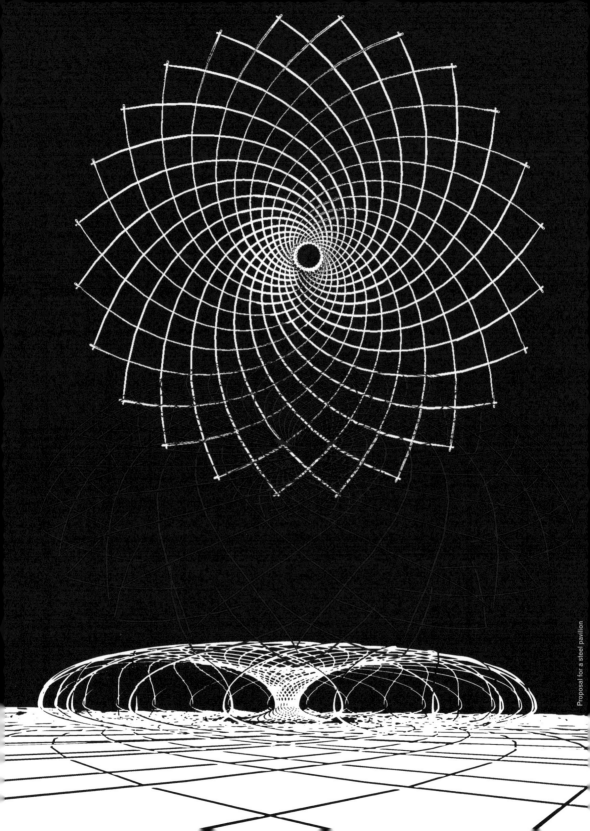

Proposal for a steel pavilion

Productive Ambiguity

Ilka and Andreas Ruby

The fact that the commission for this year's Serpentine Gallery
Pavilion has been given to artist Olafur Eliasson and architect
Kjetil Thorsen of Snøhetta represents a singularity in the history of the
Pavilion project. It is the first time that an artist has been asked to
design the Pavilion together with an architect, who, which is equally
novel, does not belong to the ubiquitous guild of star architects
who have built previous Pavilions: Zaha Hadid, Daniel Libeskind with
Arup, Toyo Ito with Arup, Oscar Niemeyer, MVRDV with Arup (unrealised), Álvaro Siza and Eduardo Souto de Moura with Cecil Balmond –
Arup, and Rem Koolhaas and Cecil Balmond, with Arup. With the
exception of the modernist legend Niemeyer, for whom the Pavilion
was more like a lifetime-achievement award, all are highly regarded
figures belonging to the contemporary star architecture system.
One could have continued the list with other members of that species:
Frank Gehry, Jean Nouvel, Kazuo Sejima, Peter Zumthor, etc. But
somehow, the Koolhaas Pavilion created a rupture, an exception to the
rule too powerful to ignore thereafter. The Pavilion project by Eliasson
and Thorsen suggests that the Serpentine Gallery, inspired by the
experience of Koolhaas's project, wanted to make sure to continue that
level of experimentation within the format of the commission itself.

Like no other architect today, Koolhaas stands for an expanded
notion of architecture – one that understands building not as the
essence of architecture, but only as one form among many with which
it can materialise its transformation of social space. Moreover,
Koolhaas belongs to a minority of architects who use writing as a part
of their practice. In fact, he was a writer before becoming an architect,
much like the movie directors of the French Nouvelle Vague such as
Jean-Luc Godard, François Truffaut and others, who originally started
out as film critics but ultimately discovered that making films was
a more effective form of criticising cinema.

This operative approach to criticism became clearly visible in the
discursive programming of the 2006 Pavilion, which was one of
its constituent elements. Treating discourse almost as a conceptual
building material, the Koolhaas Pavilion took a very different
approach from any of its predecessors. While most of them celebrated,
and evolved, the tradition of the pavilion as a sort of light-minded,
playful alter ego of architecture, a welcome time out from the
power-inflicted reality of large-scale building, the Koolhaas Pavilion

[top]
Olafur Eliasson, *The mediated motion,*
2001, Kunsthaus Bregenz, Austria,
in collaboration with landscape architect
Günther Vogt
[right]
Olafur Eliasson, *The weather project,*
The Unilever Series, Turbine Hall,
Tate Modern, London, 2003

(which did all of that as well) tried to invent a space for discourse that reinstated and merged previous typologies of public exchange such as the agora, the *salon* or the club. Maybe the only exception to this politics of transgression was the cultural division of labour between Koolhaas's building and the art installation of Thomas Demand. This is exactly where Serpentine has gone one crucial step further this time, by entrusting Eliasson and Thorsen with the design of the Pavilion without attributing separate roles to artist and architect.

This generosity of the brief is particularly accommodating for Eliasson, since it allows him to realise to an unprecedented degree his trajectory of appropriating the language of architecture in his work. Throughout his career, Eliasson has been attracted to architecture in a number of ways, including the issue of scale. He likes to execute his installations in quasi-architectural dimensions, often custom-tailored to fit particular buildings. Yet instead of simply adding a decorative sculptural object, he always seeks to transform the appearance and performance of the chosen building completely, as can be seen in *The mediated motion,* Kunsthaus Bregenz, 2001, or in *The weather project,* Tate Modern, 2003. Recently, he has even gone so far as to take over entire parts of buildings yet to be built, such as in the Icelandic National Concert and Conference Centre, Reykjavik (expected completion in 2009), by Henning Larsen Architects, where he is designing the entire glass facade of the building. The artwork becomes totally inseparable from the building as it borrows from the architectural body to materialise itself.

The Serpentine Gallery Pavilion represents a significant moment in Eliasson's work because it is here, for the first time, that the disciplinary and material interface between art and architecture has become ultimately invisible – an achievement for which co-author Thorsen cannot be credited enough. Indeed, Thorsen and Eliasson have managed to synchronise their efforts to such a degree that there is no dividing line between the artist's and the architect's contribution; no marking of territories, because there are no separate territories to begin with – the Pavilion is just one entity, object, building or whatever you wish to call it.

If we compare the Serpentine Pavilion project to Eliasson's previous excursion into pavilions, the *Your black horizon Art Pavilion* commissioned by Thyssen-Bornemisza Art Contemporary from Eliasson and architect David Adjaye, we can see that this is a new quality in his work. Even though the collaboration between the artist and architect appears to have been seamless, the resulting project

[top]
Olafur Eliasson, visualisation of glass brick façade for the Icelandic National Concert and Conference Centre, Reykjavik, Iceland, 2007, due for completion 2009
[opposite, top]
Snøhetta, *Ras Al-Khaimah-Gateway project,* Ras Al-Khaimah, United Arab Emirates, schematic design 2007
[opposite, bottom]
Snøhetta, *National Opera House,* Oslo, Norway, due for completion 2008

Adjaye/Associates, *Your black horizon Art Pavilion,* 51st Venice Biennale, 2005

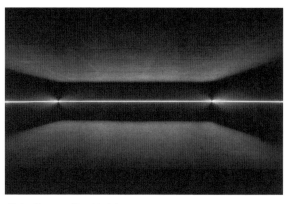

Olafur Eliasson, *Your black horizon,* 51st Venice Biennale, 2005

clearly reads as two material parts, however interconnected. Eliasson created the light installation *Your black horizon,* 2005, and Adjaye designed the pavilion around it. While both parts clearly respond in dialogue, they also maintain a respectful distance, granting each other relative autonomy. And they remain in an 'either-or' dialectic: depending on whether you are inside or outside, you can either see the light installation or the architectural pavilion, but never both at the same time. With the Serpentine Pavilion, Eliasson for the first time ventures into the realm of a stand-alone building that confronts the viewer with art as building (and no longer inside one) – a condition that would correspond to what Robert Venturi called the principle of the 'both-and' as opposed to the 'either-or'.[1]

It will be an adventure to view the consequences of this crucial move in his work. Even without being able to see the finished Pavilion, which is taking shape while this text is being written, it is obvious that the explicitly architectural nature of the object gives Eliasson a much more direct grip on his appropriation of architecture. It is almost as if by inhabiting the object typology of a building, he can now *absorb* architecture as a cultural practice, and appropriate some of its operative properties.

One of those properties is context. Architecture is always confronted with context. A building invariably stands in a specific place, which it cannot escape, unlike most art, which has cultivated the museum as its non site-specific, global logistic condition, thanks to the white cube as a universal neutralising exhibition context. In his previous work, Eliasson had already showed a strong interest in transgressing the Truman-Show-effect of the museum, by reprogramming its space as a host condition to be colonised by the real. Or he would use the opposite strategy, abandoning the museum as a context altogether and colonising the real through temporal art interventions such as *Green river*, 1998, or *Erosion*, 1997. The Eliasson/Thorsen Pavilion is an installation on the scale of a building that addresses its context via a series of interconnected conditions reminiscent of a set of Chinese boxes: the Pavilion relates to the Serpentine Gallery building, which relates to Kensington Gardens and the neighbouring Hyde Park, which relate to London and so on. Each element of this sequence refers to a former self that reveals a

1   Robert Venturi, *Complexity and Contradiction in Architecture* (New York: Museum
     of Modern Art Books, 1966), 22–23: 'I am for messy vitality over obvious unity ...
     I am for richness of meaning rather than clarity of meaning ... I prefer "both-and" to
     "either-or," black and white, and sometimes gray, to black or white'

displacement of its original function: the Pavilion by Eliasson and
Thorsen refers to its precedents that were designed by architects only;
the Gallery building refers to its original function as a teahouse,
now popular outdoor hang-out spot of adjacent Hyde Park resonates
with its history as the location of the Great Exhibition in 1851,
the mother of all later world exhibitions, and the site of Crystal Palace,
a building that revolutionised the world of architecture, although –
or because – it was designed by an engineer who had previously
mostly built greenhouse structures. This in turn refers back to
the series of previous Serpentine Pavilions that for the most part have
involved Cecil Balmond, Deputy Chairman of Arup and Arup Fellow,
a structural engineer who prefers to refer to himself as a 'structural
designer', which brings us back again to the trope of the merging
of disciplines. Indeed, the iterations of references and content
relationships that Eliasson/Thorsen are able to address due to the
physical and historical nature of the Pavilion's context seem infinitely
bigger than those offered by the deterritorialised space of
the museum.

Being a building, even if co-designed by an artist and realised in
an art context, the Pavilion is inevitably contextualised in the field
of architecture. Every move resonates with a whole history of buildings,
typologies and architectural paradigms. Eliasson and Thorsen are
aware of this, and decided to jump on this referential trampoline with
full force. Thus the entire Pavilion becomes a meta-discourse on
architecture, processing some of its crucial archetypes, and one in
particular: the spiralling ramp. Throughout the history of architecture,
the spiral has been used as a metaphor for evolution and time,
and, in Modernism, also for progress. We can see this from the Tower
of Babel to Tatlin's tower and Frank Lloyd Wright's Solomon R.

Pieter Bruegel the Elder, *The Tower of Babel,* 1563

Vladimir Tatlin, *Model of the Monument
to the Third International,* 1920

Guggenheim Museum – all of which had to face the paradox, that, although based on an essentially infinite geometric figure, they had to come to an end at some point due to the building's finite condition. They each dealt with the paradox in different ways: Babel was never finished, Tatlin's tower never built, and Wright basically ended the Guggenheim spiral ramp with an anticlimax (it simply stops in the shape of a larger gallery). Wright's building in particular features a staggering inversion of meaning: intended to evoke evolution, the building ends up monumentalising the entropy of history. His spiral reigned over architecture for decades as the prototypical cliché of continuity, replicated in a number of architectural derivations repeating its dilemma. A breakthrough was reached only as late as 1992 with the legendary design for the Bibliothèques de Jussieu in Paris by OMA / Rem Koolhaas. This unbuilt proposal sought to overcome the linear time of the spiral by mutating into a folded landscape that spirals its way up and down as a continuous surface with an overall itinerary of 1.5 km in length.

In their Serpentine Pavilion, Eliasson and Thorsen use the technique of an imaginary continuation of the ramp that presents a striking inversion of the classical concept of the 'borrowed view' from English gardens. To understand the impact of this inversion, we might look at an implementation of that concept in one of the most influential houses of the 20th century, Le Corbusier's Villa Savoye in Poissy, France, 1930. To facilitate a seamless movement through the building by means of a *promenade architecturale,* Le Corbusier replaced stairs wherever possible with one central ramp, which connects ground level, first floor and rooftop in a single movement. To resolve the problem of the end, he led the ramp to a wall, which is punched through with a picture window framing the natural

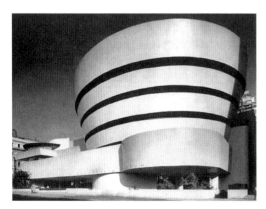

Frank Lloyd Wright, *Solomon R. Guggenheim Museum,* New York, 1959

OMA / Rem Koolhaas, *Jussieu – Two Libraries Competition,* Paris, 1992

surroundings of the place. Thus the finite movement of the ramp, which has to come to a halt where the building stops, is continued in the projective vector of our gaze. The Eliasson/Thorsen Pavilion repeats this gesture, but completely redirects it by letting the ramp end in a balcony that punctures the inclined roof of the Pavilion to give a view of the space inside. In this way, the upward movement of the ramp does not end, but goes back to an earlier moment of its evolution, which is the space inside the Pavilion, actually its only room. While Le Corbusier tries to realise the spiral's promise of infinity through a projection into nature, or the universe for that matter, the Eliasson/Thorsen Pavilion proposes a logic of evolution known from cognitive science and radical Constructivism and one of the recurrent modes of thinking in Eliasson's art — recursive iteration, evident in his oft-quoted motif 'seeing oneself seeing'. Conceived as an expanded section of the ramp, this dome-shaped space is reluctant to fit too easily into any typological drawer.

It is this ambiguity that harbours the project's biggest potential: to provide a space ambiguous enough not to be constraining, but specific enough to encourage scenarios of appropriation by its users — a balance that is proper to Eliasson's work in general. But ultimately the importance of the Pavilion reaches well beyond its authors. One could argue that by choosing an artist and architect to design the Pavilion, the Serpentine wanted to acknowledge a tendency in art that has emerged over the last 15 years, of which Eliasson is but one representative. One could name Jorge Pardo with his (sometimes permanent) architectural installations such as his Pavilion for the Skulpturenprojekte Münster 1997 and his house in Los Angeles; or the temporary transformations of buildings by Santiago Sierra, like the Kunsthaus Bregenz, 2004, or the Spanish Pavilion in the Giardini

Le Corbusier, *Villa Savoye,* Poissy-sur-Seine, France, 1929

of the 50th Venice Biennale in 2003; or the architectural metamorphosis that Gregor Schneider applied to his *Haus Ur,* 1985–2007, amongst many others. All of these have, in different ways, incorporated architecture as part of their material and conceptual vocabulary. After decades of alienation and forced marriages such as *Kunst am Bau,*[2] art and architecture are now relating in a productive ambiguity in which the effect has priority over the technique that helped it to occur. We have grown accustomed to situations of disciplinary cross-dressing such as art that looks like a building or, vice versa, architecture that looks like a work of art.

Indeed, we can see the same process of transgression in recent architecture. Over the past decade or two, a number of architects have consistently integrated art – as a discourse, not as an object – into their material and conceptual vocabulary. The most iconic example of this development is Diller Scofidio's Blur Building for Expo.02 in Yverdon-les-Bains, Switzerland, 2002, an exhibition pavilion sited on a lake that did not exhibit anything, but instead produced fog that wrapped its structure, wetted its visitors and obscured their vision. The work of French architect François Roche of R&Sie(n) is another example of art and architecture becoming partners in crime without even delineating these territories. Roche has repeatedly worked with contemporary artists such as Philippe Parreno and Pierre Huyghe on projects that broke new ground for both art and architecture. At Rirkrit Tiravanija's artists' community The Land in Chiang Mai, Thailand, he built a pavilion that could generate electrical energy with the aid of a local buffalo. The structure was not, however,

2   'Art applied to architecture', a governmental subsidiary programme in Germany obliging clients of public buildings to spend 1% of the building budget on artworks applied to the building

Diller Scofidio, *Blur Building,* Swiss Expo,
Neuchâtel, Switzerland, 2002

François Roche and Philippe Parreno, *The Game,* 2003

R&Sie(n), *Hybrid Muscle (the movie which create a shelter)*
Philippe Parreno, *Boys from Mars (the shelter which create a movie)*

conceived as an autonomous building, but as a backdrop for a fake documentary on Thailand made by Parreno in the tradition of the faked ethnological films of Robert Flaherty. But even in his buildings done without the participation of artists, Roche consistently employs conceptual strategies that are more familiar in the artistic field than in architecture. This allows his projects to explore an exceptionally rich conceptual territory: a school of architecture in Venice that sucks up the water of the Lagoon; a museum of art in Bangkok that attracts the dust out of the polluted air by virtue of its electrically charged metal facade; or a pedestrian bridge over a river between Poland and the Czech Republic that maximises the chances of its users (potentially alcoholised) to get lost on their way home late at night ...

This complicity of art and architecture increasingly breeds professional practices that no longer fit exactly into either category, but remain compatible with both. realities:united is a representative of this tendency, a Berlin-based media/architecture office led by Jan & Tim Edler, who tune buildings by manipulating their hardware, and hence their performance, with installations on an architectural scale, such as their 900 metre-square media facade of Kunsthaus Graz, which made their name on an international level. In 2006, they were asked to develop a temporary 'stand-in' during the one year-renovation period of Museum Abteiberg in Mönchengladbach, built in 1975 by Hans Hollein, which initiated the museum boom of the 1980s and, according to Frank Gehry, even anticipated the Bilbao-effect. Instead of a stand-alone structure like a 'pavilion' realities:united chose to squat an existing building, Mönchengladbach's former City Theatre, which had been standing empty for a couple of years due to lack of communal funds. The once beautiful Modernist building was derelict, earmarked for demolition and soon to be replaced by a new shopping centre.

realities:united, *Museum X,* Interim for the Museum Abteiberg, Mönchengladbach, Germany, 2006

realities:united covered the main façade of the 1960s theatre building
with identical panels of PVC foil, inkjet-printed with a photograph
of exposed aggregate to evoke the look of a typical museum building
from the 1960s, an impression reinforced by a name-plate fixed to
the fake façade reading 'MUSEUM'. Its only accessible space was the
foyer, which quoted Hollein's famous neon-lamp ceiling pattern,
and featured a counter and museum shop, but otherwise led nowhere.
In this way, a building that had been declared dead became a catalyst
for a discussion in the city on the role of culture and shopping
in its future urban development. Though hardly more than a phantom,
the building has managed to transform the urban space of the city:
the bus stop next to it has been renamed 'Museum X' (the project's title),
and the plaza is now better maintained for the convenience of those
who stop and contemplate the unexpected monument. In a purely
architectural methodology, this type of semiotic building would have
been unthinkable and likely to be dismissed as a Potemkinian village,
or as flat-out un-architectural. However, in the expanded field of
aesthetic practice created through those curious liaisons of artists and
architects (and, needless to add, practitioners of other disciplines),
this kind of operation becomes viable.

Likewise, an operation like the Serpentine Gallery Pavilion 2007
could only have taken shape thanks to a consistent exploration
of the politics surrounding the transgression of established notions
of art, including its material strategies, its institutional conditions
and the role and position that art should take within today's
mass-media-driven event culture. While there is clearly no single
answer, it is crucial to pose and explore these questions. The new
Serpentine Gallery Pavilion might just be the right kind of environment
in which to host that inquiry.

Olafur Eliasson
Selected Biography

1967 born in Copenhagen, Denmark
1989–1995 studied at the Royal
    Danish Academy of Fine Arts,
    Copenhagen
lives in Berlin, Germany,
    and Copenhagen, Denmark

Selected Projects and
Permanent Installations

2009
Glass brick for the façade of the
    Icelandic National Concert and
    Conference Centre, commissioned
    by Portus group of Reykjavik,
    architecture by Henning Larsen
    Architects, Reykjavik, Iceland
2008
Foyer installation for National Opera
    House, Oslo, Norway
2007
Your black horizon Art Pavilion,
    with David Adjaye, commissioned
    by Thyssen-Bornemisza Art
    Contemporary (T-B A 21),
    Lopud Island, Croatia
2006
Light lab (2006–08), Portikus,
    Frankfurt, Germany
2004
Camera Obscura für die Donau,
    commissioned by Kunst im
    Öffentlichen Raum Niederöster-
    reich und Arbeitskreis Wachau,
    Rollfähre Spitz, Arnsdorf, Austria
Dufttunnel, Autostadt GmbH
    Wolfsburg, Germany
Umschreibung, KPMG corporate
    headquarters, Munich, Germany
2003
Sphere, commissioned by
    Hypo-Vereinsbank, Fünf Höfe,
    Munich, Germany

2002
Lichtvorhang and *Mooswand*
    (collaboration with
    Baumschlager + Eberle),
    Münchener Rückversicherungs-
    gesellschaft, Munich, Germany
Quasi brick wall, Fundación NMAC,
    Cádiz, Spain
2001
Windspiegelwand, Deutsche
    Gesellschaft für Technische
    Zusammenarbeit (GTZ), Berlin,
    Germany
2000
Der drehende Park, Sammlung
    Kunstwegen, Nordhorn, Germany
The movement meter for Lernacken,
    Malmö, Sweden

Selected Exhibitions

2007
Take your time, San Francisco
    Museum of Modern Art, travelling
    to The Museum of Modern Art and
    P.S.1 Contemporary Art Center,
    New York, USA
2006
*Your uncertainty of colour matching
    experiment* (in cooperation with
    Boris Oicherman), Ikon Gallery,
    Birmingham, UK
*Eye on Europe: Prints, Books &
    Multiples / 1960 to Now,*
    The Museum of Modern Art,
    New York, USA (group exhibition)
2005
Your light shadow, Hara Museum
    of Contemporary Art, Tokyo, Japan
Notion motion, Museum Boijmans
    van Beuningen, Rotterdam,
    Netherlands
Here Comes the Sun, Magasin 3
    Stockholm Konsthall, Sweden
    (group exhibition)
2004
Your Lighthouse, Works with Light
    1991–2004, Kunstmuseum
    Wolfsburg, Germany
Photographs, The Menil Collection,
    Houston, USA
2003
The weather project, The Unilever
    Series, Turbine Hall, Tate Modern,
    London, UK

The blind pavilion, Danish Pavilion,
    50th Venice Biennale, Italy
Utopia Station, 50th Venice Biennale,
    Italy (group exhibition)
2002
*Chaque matin je me sens différent,
    chaque soir je me sens le même,*
    Musée d'Art moderne de la Ville de
    Paris, France
*Claude Monet ... bis zum digitalen
    Impressionismus,* Fondation
    Beyeler, Riehen, Switzerland
    (group exhibition)
2001
The mediated motion (collaboration
    with Günther Vogt), Kunsthaus
    Bregenz, Austria
*Projects 73: Olafur Eliasson: seeing
    yourself sensing,* The Museum of
    Modern Art, New York, USA
2000
Surroundings surrounded,
    Neue Galerie am Landesmuseum
    Joanneum, Graz, Austria
1999
Carnegie International, 1999/2000,
    Carnegie Museum of Art,
    Pittsburgh, USA (group exhibition)
*German Open: Gegenwartskunst
    in Deutschland,* Kunstmuseum
    Wolfsburg, Germany
    (group exhibition)
d'APERTutto, 48th Venice Biennale,
    Italy (group exhibition)
1998
Berlin / Berlin – 1. Berlin Biennale,
    Akademie der Künste;
    Postfuhramt; KW Institute for
    Contemporary Art, Berlin,
    Germany (group exhibition)
1997
The curious garden, Kunsthalle
    Basel, Switzerland

Kjetil Trædal Thorsen
Selected Biography

1958 born in Haugesund, Norway
1977–1985 studied architecture
  at the Technical University,
  Graz, Austria

1987
co-founder of Snøhetta Arkitektur
  Landskap
1990
co-founder of Snøhetta AS
2004–
Professor at University of Innsbruck,
  Austria
lives and works in Oslo, Norway

Selected Projects (completion date)

2009–
National Academy of the Arts,
  Bergen, Norway, with Norwegian
  National Building Authority
  representing the Ministry of
  Education as client
WTC Museum and Visitor Center,
  Ground Zero, New York, USA,
  with Memorial Foundation as client
University Campus at Faraba Banta,
  The Gambia, with Ministry
  of Higher Education as client
Ras Al Khaimah Gateway, UAE,
  with Rakeen as client
Vivaldi buildings, Zuidas, Amsterdam,
  Holland, with Bleuwhood and
  ING as clients
2008
National Opera House, Oslo,
  Norway, with Norwegian National
  Building Authority representing the
  Ministry of Culture as client
Lysaker Train Station, Oslo, Norway,
  with Jernbaneverket as client

2007
Five art pavilions for Kivik Art Centre,
  Sweden, with Tom Sandberg,
  commissioned by the Kivik Art
  Centre Foundation
Petter Dass Museum, Allstahaug,
  Norway, commissioned by
  Petter Dass KF
Eggum Visitor Centre,
  Vestvågøy, Norway
2006
Music pavilion for Kongsberg Jazz
  Festival, Norway, with Kongsberg
  Jazz Festival as client
2005
City lights of Skien, Norway,
  with Commune of Skien as client
2004
Mediterranean Institiute for
  Neurobiology, Marseille, France,
  with Inserm as client
Frame, bus shelters in Trondheim,
  Norway, commissioned by Adshel
2003
Sandvika Cultural Centre, Norway,
  with the Commune of Sandvika
  as client
Drøbak Town Centre, Norway, with
  the Commune of Drøbak as client
2002
Bibliotheca Alexandrina, Alexandria,
  Egypt, with Ministry of Higher
  Education as client
The Contemporary Tube,
  The Contemporary Museum of
  Norway, Oslo, commissioned
  by the Museum Restaurant SANS,
  Oslo, Norway, commissioned by
  the owners
2001
Hamar Townhall, Hamar, Norway,
  with the Commune of Hamar
  as client
ARTESIA Spa, Oslo, Norway,
  commissioned by the owner
2000
Zumtobel Staff Showroom, Sandvika,
  Norway, with Zumtobel Staff
  as client
Norwegian Embassy in Berlin,
  Germany, with Ministry of Foreign
  Affairs as client
The Garden of Bjørnson, Oslo,
  Norway, with several clients

1999–1990
Karmøy Fishing Museum, Karmøy,
  Norway, commissioned by Karmøy
  Fishing Museum Foundation
Skistua School, Narvik, Norway,
  with the Commune of Narvik
  as client
The Streets of Longyearbyen,
  Svalbard, with Authority of
  Svalbard as client
The Czech Embassy in Oslo, Norway,
  commissioned by the Ministry
  of Foreign Affairs
Lillehammer Art Museum for the
  Winter Olympics, Norway
Lillehammer Station for the Winter
  Olympics, Norway
The Park of Vaterland, Oslo, Norway
Sonja Hennies Park, Oslo, Norway

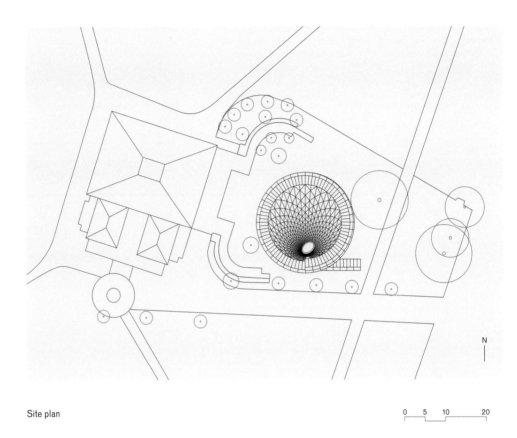

N

Site plan

0   5   10   20

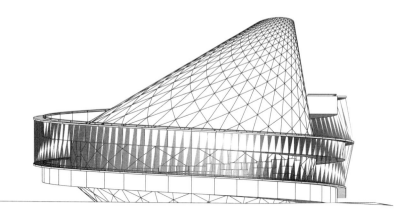

West Elevation

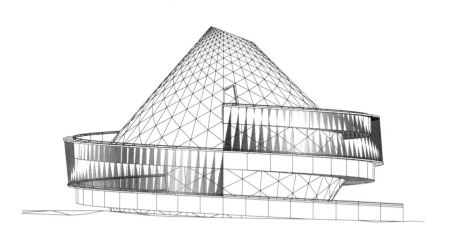

South Elevation

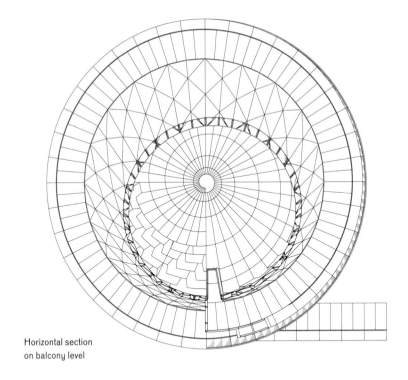

Horizontal section
on balcony level

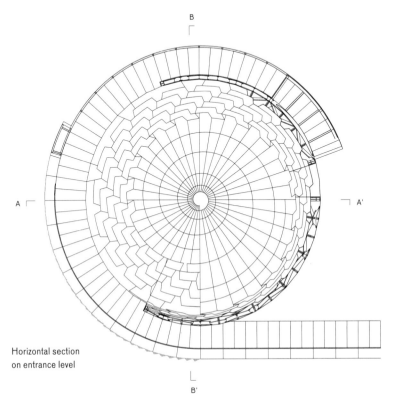

B

A ⌐   ⌐ A'

B'

Horizontal section
on entrance level

118

Vertical section AA'

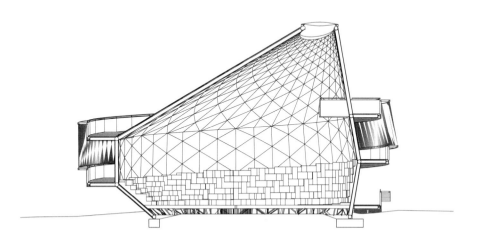

Vertical section BB'

0   1   5   10

Author Biographies

Doreen Massey has been Professor of
Geography at the Open University
since 1982. She has written widely about
space, place, cities, globalisation and
regional inequality. Her books include
Capital and Land, 1978, *Spatial Divisions
of Labour,* 1984, *High-tech Fantasies* 1992,
Space, Place and Gender, 1994 and
*Power-geometries and the Politics
of Space-time,* 1999, *For Space,* 2005
and most recently *World City,* 2007.

Andreas Ruby is an architectural
theorist and Ilka Ruby is an architect and
graphic designer. In 2001, they set
up 'textbild' — an agency for architectural
communication operating in the fields of
publishing, curating, teaching and consulting.
They have written an designed
a number of books about contemporary
architecture, including *Minimal Architecture,*
2003, *Images. A Picture Book of Architecture,* 2004, *Groundscapes,* 2005, and
Dominique Perrault: Meta-Buildings, 2006.
They regularly lecture at architecture
schools worldwide and currently teach at
the Berlin University of the Arts and
the Metropolis Program of the Universitat
Politècnica de Catalunya in Barcelona.

Pavilion Team

Architecture
Olafur Eliasson
Kjetil Thorsen

Design Team
Ben Allen, *SOE, Architect*
Sebastian Behmann, *SOE, Senior Architect*
Andreas Eggertsen, *Snøhetta, Architect*
Ricardo Gomes, *SOE, Project Architect*
Aase Mortensen, *Snøhetta, Senior Architect*

Visualisation and Production Assistance
Robert Banović, *Targa Design, Architect*
Norbert Palz, *Targa Design, Architect*

3D Modelling Assistance
Fredrik Wenstøp, *Pivot, Industrial Designer*
Kristian Wenstøp, *Pivot, Product Designer*

Assisted by
Néstor Pérez Batista, *SOE, Architect*
Erik Huber, *SOE, Lighting Architect*
Sharron Ping Jen Lee, *SOE, Architect*
Erik Nordbye, *ebn design, Architect*
Andreas Nypan, *Snøhetta, Landscape Architect*
Sven Pfeiffer, *SOE, Architect*
Joshua Teas, *Snøhetta, Architect*
Rune Veslegard, *Snøhetta, Architect*

Structural Engineering
Jörg Beierbach
Attila Bodenseh
Herwig Bretis
Switbert Greiner

Project Directors
Julia Peyton-Jones with
Hans Ulrich Obrist, *Serpentine Gallery*

Project Leader
Julie Burnell, *Serpentine Gallery*

Project Organiser
Rebecca Morrill, *Serpentine Gallery*

Project Managers
Alexander Dietrich, *Bovis Lend Lease*
Bernard Franklin, *Bovis Lend Lease*

Project Advisors
Lord Palumbo, *Chairman, Serpentine Gallery Board of Trustees*
Zaha Hadid, *Architect, Serpentine Gallery Board of Trustees*
Peter Rogers, *Director, Stanhope Plc*
Cecil Balmond, *Deputy Chairman and Arup Fellow, Arup*
Mark Robinson
Mark Camley, *Chief Executive, Royal Parks Agency*
Westminster City Council *Planning Office*
Westminster City Council District *Surveyor's Office (Building Control)*
Westminster City Council *(Licensing Authority)*
London Fire and Emergency *Planning Authority*
London Region, English Heritage
Friends of Hyde Park and Kensington Gardens

Pre-Design Consultation — Arup
Daniel Bosia
Peter Bressington
Pat Dallard
Florian Gauss
Alistair Guthrie
Martin Manning
Dorothee Richter
Becci Taylor
Mick White

Technical Services Consultation — Arup
David Deighton
Anthony Ferguson
James Thonger
Peter Williams

Contractors
Abbey Thermal (insulation)
Barr Construction (timber seating)
Bovis Lend Lease Limited (construction management and CDM co-ordinator)
The Bradley Collection (curtain fixtures and installation)
Carey Group Plc (excavation driver and landscaping works)
Clipfine (security and slinger/signaller)
CMF (metalwork)
Davis Langdon LLP (quantity surveyor)
DP9 (planning application and services)
Envirograf (timber treatment)
EMS (temporary power/water)
Gardner & Co (heating)
John Doyle Group (groundworks)
Keltbray (dismantling)
Konzept:werk (façade element)
Kvadrat (textiles and moveable seating)
Lyndon Scaffolding Plc (scaffolding and rain cover)
Nüssli (timber cladding)
Protec (fire alarms)
Rohlfing (steel structure)
SES (surveying and site set out)
Select Plant Hire Co Ltd — Cranes (site equipment)
Swift Horsman Limited (café/bar construction)
T. Clarke (small power and lighting installation)
TSK General Transport (transport: Switzerland)
Vector Foiltec (rooflight fabrication and installation)
Weil, Gotshal & Manges (legal services)
William Hare Ltd (safety netting)
Wilson James (transport: London)
Zumtobel (lighting)

Royal Commission for the
Exhibition of 1851 Foundation
Royal Norwegian Embassy
The Dr Mortimer and Theresa
Sackler Foundation

And kind assistance from
Embassy of Denmark, London
The Lone Pine Foundation
The Nyda and Oliver Prenn
Foundation
The Office for Contemporary Art
Norway
The Royal Borough of
Kensington and Chelsea
Westminster Arts
Westminster City Council

Exhibition Programme supported by
303 Gallery, New York / Lisa Spellman
Burger Collection Switzerland /
Hong Kong
Cao Fei and Lombard-Freid Projects
Calouste Gulbenkian Foundation
Center for Icelandic Art, Iceland
Frank and Cherryl Cohen
Sadie Coles / Sadie Coles HQ
Contemporary Fine Arts, Berlin
Embassy of the United States
of America, London
Fondation Cartier
pour l'art contemporain
Larry Gagosian / Gagosian Gallery
Greene Naftali Gallery, New York
Pia-Christina Miller
Galerie Urs Meile, Lucerne-Beijing
The Henry Moore Foundation
Pierre Huber
Jay Jopling / White Cube
John Kaldor and Naomi Milgrom
Lazarides Gallery
Matthew Marks Gallery
Victoria Miro Gallery
Ministry for Foreign Affairs, Iceland
Ministry of Education, Science and
Culture, Iceland
Outset Contemporary Art Fund
Parkview International London Plc
The Red Mansion Foundation
Mrs Turidur Reynisdottir
Craig Robins
Ruth and Richard Rogers
Royal Netherlands Embassy
Royal Norwegian Embassy
Novator Partners LLP
Sigurður Gisli Pálmason

Galerie Eva Presenhuber,
Zürich / Eva Presenhuber
Esther Schipper
Melissa and Robert Soros
Galerie Sprüth Magers,
Cologne, Munich / Monika Sprüth
and Philomene Magers
Julia Stoschek Foundation e.V.
David Tang
David Teiger
Guy and Myriam Ullens Foundation

Emeritus Benefactor
Edwin C Cohen and
The Blessing Way Foundation

Honorary Patron
Anthony Podesta, Podesta /
Mattoon.com, Washington DC

Honorary Benefactors
Gavin Aldred
Mark and Lauren Booth
Noam and Geraldine Gottesman
Mark Hix
Catherine and Pierre Lagrange
Stig Larsen
George and Angie Loudon
Jo and Raffy Manoukian
Des McDonald

Patrons
Abstract Select Ltd
Mrs Sigi Aiken
Mr Christian Angermayer
Dr Bettina Bahlsen
Simon Bakewell and
Cheri Phillips
Philippe and Bettina Bonnefoy
Frances Bowes
Brian Boylan
Basia and Richard Briggs
Mrs Rita Caltagirone
Laurent and Micky Caraffa
Mr and Mrs Federico Ceretti
Dr Martin A Clarke
Sir Ronald and Lady Cohen
Terence and Niki Cole
Stevie Congdon and
Harriet Hastings
Alastair Cookson
Rob and Siri Cope
Alex Dann
Robin and Noelle Doumar
Frank and Lorna Dunphy
The Edwin Fox Foundation

Mrs Carmen Engelhorn
Leonardo and Alessia Giangreco
Karine Giannamore
Chris and Jacqui Goekjian
David Gorton
Sir Ronald Grierson
Reade and Elizabeth Griffith
Mr and Mrs Habib
Marianne Holtermann and
Lance Entwistle
Dorian Jabri
Tim Jefferies
Dr Morana Jovan and
Mr George
Embiricos
Mr and Mrs Karim Juma
Pauline Karpidas
Ofir and Eva Kedar
Mr and Mrs Lahoud
Eddie and Danny Lawson
Mr Edouard Lecieux
Mr and Mrs Simon Lee
Rachel Lehmann and
David Maupin
Peder Lund
Aniz Manji
Andrew and Jacqueline Martin
Vincent and Elizabeth Meyer
Mr Donald Moore
Gregor Muir
Paul and Alison Myners
Yuki Oshima-Wilpon
Cornelia Pallavicini
Katherine Priestley and
David Pitblado
Ivan and Marina Ritossa
Hugo Rittson-Thomas
Kadee Robbins
David Roberts
Lily Safra
Alan and Joan Smith
Lord Edward Spencer-Churchill
Mr and Mrs David Stevenson
Siri Stolt-Nielsen
Ian and Mercedes Stoutzker
Laura and Barry Townsley
Melissa Ulfane
Dr Vera Vucelic
Peter Wheeler and
Pascale Revert
Benedict Wilkinson and
Mia Spence
Mr Samer Younis and
Mrs Rana Sadik
Poju and Anita Zabludowicz
Riccardo Zacconi

123

Britt Lintner
Barbara Lloyd and
    Judy Collins
Sotiris TF Lyritzis
Steve and Fran Magee
Mr Otto Julius Maier and
    Mrs Michèle Claudel-Maier
Claude Mandel and
    Maggie Mechlinski
Cat Martin
Mr and Mrs Stephen Mather
Viviane and James Mayor
Alexandra Meyers
Warren and Victoria Miro
Susan and Claus Moehlmann
Jen Moores
Gillian Mosely
Richard Nagy and
    Caroline Schmidt
Andrei Navrozov
Angela Nikolakopoulou
Dalit Nuttall
Georgia Oetker
Sandra and Stephan Olajide
Tamiko Onozawa
Mr and Mrs Nicholas Oppenheim
Linda Pace
Desmond Page and
    Asun Gelardin
Maureen Paley
Dominic Palfreyman
Midge and Simon Palley
Kathrine Palmer
Andrew and Jane Partridge
Julia Peyton-Jones
George and Carolyn Pincus
Lauren Papadopoulos Prakke
Victoria Preston
Sophie Price
Mathew Prichard
Max Reed
Michael Rich
John and Jill Ritblat
Bruce and Shadi Ritchie
Kasia Robinski
Kimberley Robson-Ortiz Foundation
Jacqueline and Nicholas Roe
Victoria, Lady de Rothschild
James Roundell and
    Bona Montagu
Rolf and Maryam Sachs
Nigel and Annette Sacks
Michael and Julia Samuel
Ronnie and Vidal Sassoon
Joana and Henrik Schliemann
Glenn Scott Wright

The Selvaag Family
Nick Simou and
    Julie Gatland
Mr and Mrs Jean-Marc Spitalier
Bina and Philippe von Stauffenberg
Tanya and David Steyn
Simone and Robert Suss
Emma Tennant and
    Tim Owens
The Thames Wharf Charity
Christian and Sarah
    von Thun-Hohenstein
Britt Tidelius
Suzanne Togna
Emily Tsingou
JP Ujobai
Ashley and Lisa Unwin
David and Emma Verey
Darren J Walker
Audrey Wallrock
Offer Waterman
Rajan and Wanda Watumull
Pierre and Ziba de Weck
Daniel and Cecilia Weiner
Alannah Weston
Helen Ytuarte White
Robin Wight and
    Anastasia Alexander
Martha and David Winfield
Mr and Mrs M Wolridge
Chad Wollen and
    Sian Davies
Nabil N Zaouk
Andrzej and Jill Zarzycki

And Patrons, Future Contemporaries
and Benefactors who wish to remain
anonymous

International Media Partner
Fortune

125

Published to accompany
the Serpentine Gallery Pavilion 2007
by Olafur Eliasson and Kjetil Thorsen
August – November 2007

Catalogue compiled by
Caroline Eggel and
Anna Engberg-Pedersen,
    Studio Olafur Eliasson
Ben Fergusson and
Rebecca Morrill,
    Serpentine Gallery

Edited by Melissa Larner

Designed by Michael Heimann and
Hendrik Schwantes, Berlin

Printing:
Jütte-Messedruck GmbH, Leipzig

Binding:
Kunst- und Verlagsbuchbinderei
GmbH, Leipzig

ISBN 978-3-03778-116-6
Lars Müller Publishers

ISBN 978-1-905190-17-1
Serpentine Gallery

Lars Müller Publishers
5400 Baden, Switzerland
www.lars-mueller-publishers.com

Serpentine Gallery
Kensington Gardens
London, W2 3XA
T +44 (0)20 7402 6075
F +44 (0)20 7402 4103
www.serpentinegallery.org

The Serpentine Gallery
is supported by

Photographic credits

All images © 2007
Cover image, pp 2, 11 (right), 41–73
    Luke Hayes Photography
p 8 (left) Dafydd Jones
p 8 (right) Hélène Binet
p 9 (left) Stephen White
p 9 (right) Michel Moch
p 10 (right) Richard Bryant/
    arcaid.co.uk
p 11 (left) John Offenbach
pp 15, 102 (bottom) Jens Ziehe
p 19 Mark Robinson
pp 20, 21 (bottom), 23–25, 28–30,
    33, 34, 36, 37, 39, 40
    Ludwig Abache
pp 21 (top), 22 Studio Olafur Eliasson
p 102 (top) Markus Tretter
p 104 Cameraphoto Arte,
    Venezia / T-B A 21
p 107 (left) akg images, Erich Lessing
p 107 (right) bpk
p 108 (left) Roger Wood / CORBIS
p 108 (right) Hans Werlemann
p 109 Ilka and Andreas Ruby,
    FLC / ProLitteris, Zurich
p 110 (left) Ilka and Andreas Ruby
p 111 Natalie Czech

Comparative images

p 102 (top) Courtesy
    neugerriemschneider, Berlin
p 102 (bottom) Courtesy the artist;
    Tanya Bonakdar Gallery, New York;
    neugerriemschneider, Berlin
p 104 (top) Commissioned by Portus
    group of Reykjavik, architecture by
    Henning Larsen Architects
p 104 (bottom left) Courtesy Thyssen-
    Bornemisza Art Contemporary
    (T-B A 21), Vienna
p 104 (bottom right) Courtesy
    Thyssen-Bornemisza Art
    Contemporary (T-B A 21), Vienna
p 105 (top) Client: RAKEEN,
    Courtesy Snøhetta
p 105 (bottom) Client: Norwegian
    National Building Authority
    representing the Ministry of
    Culture, Courtesy Snøhetta

Sponsored by

Bloomberg

Design

Studio Olafur Eliasson

Snøhetta

Advisors

ARUP

STANHOPE

Media Partners

theguardian

Structural Engineering

Dr Switbert Greiner

Steel Construction

Heinrich ROHLFING GmbH

Wood Construction

NÜSSLI

Platinum Sponsor

Bovis Lend Lease   ZUMTOBEL

Gold Sponsors

CLIPFINE Construction Support Services   DAVIS LANGDON   DP9

keltbray   WEIL, GOTSHAL & MANGES

Silver Sponsors

T. Clarke

Bronze Sponsors

barr   CAREYS   EMS   GTL Partnership

Gardner & Co   HARE STRUCTURAL ENGINEERS   JOHN DOYLE   konzept:werk

kvadrat   Protec   Select

siteco   SWIFT HORSMAN LIMITED   thebradleycollection

 vectorfoiltec